On MAKING
MENDING
and DRESSING
DOLLS

A doll's hospital of 1878
(from an old engraving)

On MAKING MENDING and DRESSING Dolls

by
CLARA HALLARD FAWCETT
with illustrations by the author

HOBBY HOUSE PRESS
4701 Queensbury Road
Riverdale, Maryland 20840
U.S.A.

Copyright 1949

H. L. LINDQUIST PUBLICATIONS

3rd Printing 1975   HOBBY HOUSE PRESS

ISBN 0-87588-105-9

Printed and Bound in the United States of America

Dedicated to my
SISTER VIOLET

CONTENTS

Chapter		Page
1.	A SIMPLE DOLL FOR A SMALL CHILD—THE RAG DOLL	1
2.	CLOTH DOLLS FOR COLLECTORS	10
3.	ON CARVING AND MODELING DOLLS	16
4.	ON MENDING DOLLS, OLD AND NEW	23
5.	THE STORY OF ALICE AND MABEL, OR THE RESTORATION OF A PARIAN BISQUE DOLL	34
6.	THE STORY OF PRIVATE ROBERT EDWARD BALL OR THE RESTORATION OF A CHINA DOLL	44
7.	SUGGESTIONS FOR NINETEENTH CENTURY DOLL COSTUMES	47
8.	CHILDREN'S CLOTHES IN THE NINETEENTH CENTURY	71
9.	ON DRESSING THE "PERIOD" DOLL	95
10.	ON MAKING DOLLS TO REPRESENT AMERICA'S FIRST LADIES	109
11.	SHOES	139
12.	SOME RARE OLD DOLLS	145
13.	REPRODUCTION DOLLS	154

ILLUSTRATIONS

Illustration Number		Page Number

1. SOCK DOLL
   - 1-a—1-d: Pattern for Making Sock Doll 2
2. BEAN BAG DOLL
   - 2-a—2-d: Patterns for Making and Dressing Bean Bag Doll 2
3. ANNE, A Simple Rag Doll 4
   - 3-a—3-d: Pattern for Making Anne 4
   - 3-e—3-i: Patterns for Clothing Anne 4
   - 3-j—3-n: Hair Styles 5
   - O-1—Q-3: Making a Wig 5
4. SUSIE, A Rag Doll Circa 1900 6
   - 4-a—4-d: Pattern for Making Susie 6
   - 4-f: Susie, Completed 7
     - A. A Dress for Susie 7
     - B. A Bonnet for Susie 7
     - C. Dress Pattern 8
     - D. Bonnet Pattern 8
     - E. Susie's Cap 8
     - F. Pattern for Cap 8
     - G. (A and B). Pattern for Cape and Hood 9
     - H. An Old Dress From Susie's Wardrobe 9
5. GENEVIEVE, A Nineteenth Century Rag Doll 10
   - 5-a—5-d: Pattern for Making Genevieve 11
   - A-1—A-2: A Basque for Genevieve 12
   - A-3: Pattern for Basque 13
   - A-7: Back of Basque 13
   - 8. Shoe Upper 13
   - 9. Sole of Shoe 13
   - 10. Completed Shoe 13
   - C. A Skirt for Genevieve 13
   - 11. Skirt Pattern 20
6. WINIFRED, A Wire-Framed Doll 14
   - 6-a: Wire Frame and Padding 14
   - 6-b: Slip Covering for Head 14
7. DOROTHY, A Doll Carved by Claire Fawcett 16
   - 7-1: Carving Tools 16
   - 7-a—7-c. Parts of Carved Doll 16
8. SU-SU, A Doll with Carved Head, Arms and Legs, Stuffed Body, by Claire Fawcett 18

Illustration Number		Page Number
9.	SILLY, THE CLOWN, by Claire Fawcett	18
	9-a: Pattern for Silly's Costume	18
10.	GEORGE, A Doll Modeled by Clara Hallard Fawcett	20
11.	CARLOTTA, THE CLOTHESPIN LADY	20
	a-d: Making a Mold	21
12.	JEAN—Before and After	23
13.	JENNIE, An Old Papiér Mâché-Headed Doll Restored	24
14.	EDITHA, A Restored China-Headed Doll	25
15.	MARY ANN (China-Head) AND HER MENDED FOOT	26
16.	ATROCIA (Wax) BECOMES CECELIA	27
	16-c: A Dress For Cecelia	28
17.	GERALDINE, A Jointed Doll	29
	17-a: Geraldine in Sixteen Parts	30
	17-b: Restringing Geraldine	30
	17-c: Tools Used in Re-stringing Dolls	30
18.	DOROTHY DEE, A French Jointed Doll in Original Outfit	31
19.	TOMMY, A Bisque Swivel Head Which Needed a Body	32
	19-a: How Tommy Was Fitted Together	32
	19-b: Clothes for Tommy	33
20.	ALICE AND MABEL, Twin Dolls	34
	20-a: Pattern for Alice's Body	37
	20-b: Mending the Shoulder	37
	20-c (1-3): Chemise, Pants, Petticoat	38
	20-d: Embroidery on Alice's Best Petticoat	39
	20-e: Embroidery on Mabel's Best Petticoat	39
	20-f: A Princess Dress for the Twin	40
	20-g: Pattern for Princess Dress	40
	20-h (1 and 2): A Basque Outfit for the Twin	40
	20-h-3 (a, b, c): Pattern for Basque	40
	20-i (1 and 2): Another Basque Outfit	42
	20-i-3: Pattern for the Second Basque Outfit	42
	20-j: A Quilt for Alice	41
21.	MABEL IN PERSON	43
22.	ALICE IN PERSON	43
23.	PRIVATE ROBERT EDWARD BALL	45
	23-a: Body Pattern	45
	23-b: Leg	45
	23-(c-k): Pattern for "Soldier Boy" Outfit	45

Illustration Number		Page Number
24.	GIGOT SLEEVES OF THE 1830's FROM AN OLD SKETCH	48
25.	(1 and 2): 1. EVENING DRESS. 2. WALKING DRESS. From Godey's "Lady's Book," 1828	48
26.	COSTUME OF 1835. ANNE S. STEVENS, Editor of "The Portland Magazine," 1835	49
27.	RIDICULOUS HAIRDOS OF THE EARLY 1830's	49
28.	THE EVOLUTION OF THE BONNET	50
29.	COSTUME OF 1840. (Head from a contemporary portrait of Queen Victoria.)	50
30.	"HOME DRESS" AND "WALKING COSTUME" OF 1850. (Head in Sketch a from a contemporary portrait of Anna Cora Mowatt Ritchie, French author and actress, 1819-1870.)	51
31.	COSTUME OF 1845. (Head from a contemporary portrait of Anne Charlotte Lynch, poet.)	51
32.	GINGHAM DRESS OF 1850. Bodice was usually pointed at center waist-line instead of straight, as shown	53
33.	EVENING DRESS OF 1850. (Head from a contemporary sketch of Jenny Lind.)	53
34.	COSTUME OF 1850. (Head from a contemporary portrait of Eugenie, Empress of the French.)	54
35.	"FASHIONS FOR EARLY SUMMER." Sketched from "Harper's New Monthly Magazine," 1850. Fig. 1. Ball Dress with Apron trimming. Fig. 2. "Body" Open in Front and Laced Down to the Waist. Fig. 3...Tulip Bonnet of White Silk.	56
36.	TWO STYLES FOR "HOME TOILETTE." "Harper's," 1861.	60
37.	"SPRING PARDESSUS" (left) and "SPRING PELISSE," 1861	59
38.	"PROMENADE AND DINNER TOILETTE," 1864. Fig. 1. "Promenade Robe." Fig. 2. "Promenade Costume." Fig. 3. "Dinner Toilette."	60
39.	Fig. 1, BATHING SUITS OF THE CIVIL WAR ERA. Fig. 2, MRS. BLOOMER, 1850. FROM AN OLD SKETCH	61 61
40-43.	CARMAGO MANTLE. "Peterson's Magazine," 1868. WHITE BODY. BODY. GORED APRON.	62
44.	NURSE'S COSTUME, (taken from a sketch of Clara Barton) 1862.	63

Illustration Number		Page Number
45.	COSTUME OF 1875. Fig. 1. Street Costume. Fig. 2. A Variation of the Same, Back View.	64
46-47.	LADIES' DEMI-POLONAISE, 1875. LADIES' POINTED POSTILION BASQUE, 1875.	65
48-49	"LULU," a Cut-out from a Magazine of the 1870's Labelled by a Childish Hand. Another "PAPER DOLL" Cut-out.	65
50.	PAPER DOLL AND COSTUME OF THE 1870's.	66
51.	HEADGEAR FOR 1875 AND 1884. 1. Hat to Match Costume, 1875. 2. "Simple Hat," 1875. 3. "Velvet Bonnet," 1875. 4. Ladies' Bonnet, 1884. 5. Ladies' "Velvet Poke," 1884.	67
52-54.	DRESSES FOR PAPER DOLL CUT-OUTS OF 1888.	67
55-56.	LADIES' "STREET TOILETTE," 1895. LADIES' "DEMI-EVENING TOILETTE," 1896.	69
57-58.	WHITE BRIDAL DRESS, 1895 OR 1896. "GARDEN PARTY TOILETTE," 1895.	69
59.	A BRIDE AND HER OUTFIT CIRCA 1900.	70
60-61.	A BOY OF 1806. A GIRL OF 1813.	71
62.	A CHILD'S DRESS OF 1828. (From a contemporary picture of Princess Victoria.)	71
63.	DRESS FOR A SIX-YEAR-OLD GIRL. (From an unsigned painting dated 1833.)	72
64.	DOLL IN ORIGINAL COSTUME, CIRCA 1830.	72
65.	COSTUME FOR GIRL, 1835; BOY, 1840.	72
66.	COSTUME FOR A YOUNG GIRL, 1835. (After the painting of Princess Victoria by Sir George Hayter.)	73
67.	CHINA "YOUNG GIRL" OF THE 1850's.	74
68.	CHILDREN'S CLOTHES FROM 1850 TO 1862. No. 1. Boy's Costume of 1862. No. 2. A Girl of 1861. No. 3. A Boy's Bloomer-and-skirt Costume. No. 4. A Child's Dress of 1860. No. 5. "A Pleasing Style of Dress for a Little Boy." No. 6. "An Elegant Costume for a Little Girl." No. 7. "A Neat Costume for a Little Girl." (1850).	75

Illustration Number		Page Number
69.	CHILDREN'S COSTUMES FROM 1861 TO 1863. No. 1. A Street Dress of 1862. No. 2. A Boy and Girl of 1863. No. 3. Child's Street Dress, 1863. No. 4. Girl's Light Drab Pardessus. No. 5. Boy's Costume, 1862.	76
70.	CHILD WITH MOTHER	77
71.	CHILDREN'S DRESSES from Styles in Godey's "Lady's Book and Magazine," 1867. No. 1. Child's Dress of White Pique. No. 2. Child's Pelisse; 2-a, Muslin Body. No. 3. "Dress for a Child Just Putting on Short Clothes." No. 4. Alpaca Dress for a Little Girl.	78
72.	EIGHT WAYS OF TRIMMING CHILDREN'S DRESSES OF 1867.	79
73.	PARISIAN COSTUME FOR 1868, WITH PATTERN.	79
74.	CHINA-HEADED DOLL IN BASQUINE DRESS, Pattern for which was taken from "Peterson's Magazine" for 1868. No. 74-a: Pattern for Basquine.	80
75.	"DOLLS' DEPARTMENT." ("The Delineator," 1875.) No. 1. Chemise, pair of drawers, night-dress. No. 2. Doll's Dress. No. 3. Walking Skirt and Yoke Waist. ("The Delineator," 1884.) No. 4. Walking Skirt and Breton Jacket (1884.)	81
76.	CHINA-HEADED DOLL IN ORIGINAL COSTUME, CIVIL WAR PERIOD	81
77.	TINY CHINA-HEADED DOLL IN ORIGINAL DRESS, said to have belonged to an aunt of Abraham Lincoln.	81
78.	"VISITING DOLLS," GRACIEUSE AND ROSELEIN, Sketched from "De Deux Poupees," Paris, 1864.	82
79.	"VISITING DOLLS," MISS DARLING, NINA, PANNA MINUTKA.	82
80.	CAROL, a China-headed Doll in Dress of 1875.	83
81.	DICKIE, a China-headed Doll of 1875.	83
82.	REBECCA, a China-headed Doll of 1880.	84
83.	JAMES, a China-headed Doll Circa 1880.	84
84.	PINKIE, a Bisque-headed "Bonnet" Doll circa 1885.	84
85.	A "BONNET" HEAD OF CHINA.	84
86.	INFANT DOLL DRESS Formerly Owned by the Children of Henry Ward Beecher	85

Illustration Number		Page Number
87.	NINETEENTH CENTURY INFANT'S DRESS Owned by Mrs. Luta E. Ferrell of Washington, D. C. 87-a. Detail from Embroidered Flounce.	85
88.	OVER-DRESS ON A DOLL'S COSTUME OF 1880.	86
89.	COSTUME FOR A GIRL, 1885.	87
90.	COSTUME FOR A BOY, 1875.	87
91.	MISSES POLONAISE COSTUME.	87
92.	COSTUME FOR A FIFTEEN-YEAR-OLD, 1885.	87
93.	CAMBRIC APRON WITH RUFFLE OF EMBROIDERY FOR MISSES 8-15 YEARS OF AGE, 1875.	89
94.	APRON FOR A CHILD 2-6 YEARS OF AGE, 1875.	89
95.	MOTHER HUBBARD APRON, 2-12 YEARS OF AGE, 1885.	89
96.	APRON FOR TOT 6 MONTHS TO 3 YEARS OLD.	89
97.	APRON FOR GIRL 3-9 YEARS OF AGE.	89
98.	APRON FOR GIRL 3-9 YEARS OF AGE.	89
99.	POMPADOUR APRON FOR GIRL 3-12 YEARS OF AGE.	89
100.	LOW-NECK APRON FOR GIRL 3-12 YEARS OF AGE.	89
101.	MISSES' SACK APRON, 8-15 YEARS OF AGE.	89
102.	APRON-CLAD CHILD AND HER DOLL AND CARRIAGE.	90
103.	ORIGINAL DOLL'S APRON OF THE LATE NINETEENTH CENTURY.	90
104.	INFANT'S DRESS OF 1884.	91
105.	RAPHAEL TUCK PAPER DOLL SHOWING DRESS AND HAT OF 1894.	91
106.	RAPHAEL TUCK PAPER DOLL SHOWING UNDERWEAR, DRESS AND HAT OF 1894.	92
107.	SCHOOL DRESSES AND HATS OF 1894.	93
108.	BEACH COSTUME FOR DOLL NO. 106.	93
109.	CHANGING FORM OF SKIRT AND SLEEVE OF THE TUNICA.	95
110.	a: THE TUNICA of the Early Greeks and Romans. b: THE TUNICA TALARIS Worn as an Every-day Garment by the Clergy in the Middle of the Fourth Century.	95

Illustration Number		Page Number
111.	LATE 13TH CENTURY ATTIRE. (Head from an old engraving of Dante's Beatrice.)	96
112.	SIXTEENTH CENTURY COSTUME. (After contemporary paintings) Center, Margaret of France or Valois, 1553-1615. a: Elizabeth of Austria, 1554-1592. b: Mary Stuart, 1542-1587. c: Gabrielle of Estrees, 1571-1599. d: Louise of Lorraine, 1554-1601.	97
113.	MEN'S COSTUME IN THE LATTER HALF OF THE SIXTEENTH CENTURY.	98
114.	SEVENTEENTH CENTURY ATTIRE. (After contemporary paintings) Center, Henrietta Anne of England, 1644-1670. 1. Maria Theresa of Austria, 1638-1683. 2. Louis XIV, 1638-1715. 3. Henrietta Maria of England, 1609-1669. 4. Marie de Rohan-Montbason, 1600-1679.	99
115.	MARIE ANTOINETTE, 1755-1793. Costume Doll by Dorothy Heizer.	100
116.	LOUISE OF PRUSSIA, 1776-1810. Costume Doll by Dorothy Heizer.	100
117.	EMPRESS JOSEPHINE OF FRANCE, 1763-1814. Costume Doll by Dorothy Heizer.	100
118.	EUGENIE, EMPRESS OF FRANCE, 1826-1920. Costume Doll by Dorothy Heizer.	101
119.	CATHERINE II OF RUSSIA, 1729-1796. Costume Doll by Dorothy Heizer.	101
120.	SIX COSTUME DOLLS FROM THE METROPOLITAN MUSEUM OF ART, New York, N. Y. a: French Costume, 1420-1460. b: French Costume in the style of Mary, Queen of Scots, 1550-1590. c: German Costume, 1510-1540. d: French Costume, 1550-1558. e: English Costume, 1630-1650. f: French Costume, 1660-1680.	102
121.	TWO PORTRAIT DOLLS FROM THE TRAPHAGEN SCHOOL OF DESIGN, New York, N. Y. a: Marie Antoinette, Eighteenth Century. b: Eleanor of Toledo, Sixteenth Century.	103
122.	TWO DOLLS REPRESENTING CHARACTERS IN FICTION BY MURIEL ATKINS BRUYERE, New York, N. Y. a: Scarlett O'Hara, from the Novel, "Gone With the Wind," by Margaret Mitchell. b: "Alice in Wonderland," from the Story by Lewis Carroll.	103

Illustration Number		Page Number
123.	ALICE, Sketched From an Old Doll.	104
124.	WALKING COSTUME OF 1815. (Ensemble of Mme. Lavalette, in which her husband made his escape from prison.)	104
125.	MID-EIGHTEENTH CENTURY COSTUME. (A young Martha Washington.)	105
126.	HOOPED SKIRT OF 1740. (Revived a hundred years later in an exaggerated form.)	105
127.	COSTUME OF 1793.	106
128.	SEVENTEENTH CENTURY CHILDREN'S COSTUMES. (After the painting of Princess Mary Stewart and William II of Orange by Van Dyck.)	106
129.	CHILDREN'S COSTUMES OF 1793. (After contemporary paintings of The Dauphin and Madame Royale of France.)	107
130.	BOY'S COSTUME OF 1800. (After the painting by Goya.)	107
131.	BOY'S COSTUME OF 1892. (After a picture by John Everett Millais.)	107
132.	BOY'S COSTUME OF 1886. (After the fictional character, "Little Lord Fauntleroy," by Frances Hodgson Burnett.)	107
133.	TYPE OF DOLL BODIES POPULAR DURING THE REIGN OF THE EARLIER "FIRST LADIES." a: A Miniature "Martha Jefferson." b: A Miniature "Dolly Madison." c: A Miniature "Sarah C. Polk."	109
134.	MARTHA WASHINGTON, America's First Presiding Lady of the White House, 1789-1797.	111
135.	ABIGAIL ADAMS, Second Presiding Lady, 1797-1801.	112
136.	MARTHA JEFFERSON RANDOLPH, (Mrs. Thomas Mann Randolph) Third Presiding Lady, 1801-1809.	113
137.	DOROTHY PAINE MADISON, (Mrs. James Madison) Fourth Presiding Lady, 1809-1817.	115
138.	ELIZABETH KORTRIGHT MONROE, (Mrs. James Monroe) Fifth Presiding Lady, 1817-1825.	116
139.	MARIA HESTER MONROE GOUVERNEUR, (Mrs. Samuel Laurence Gouverneur) younger daughter of President James Monroe.	116
140.	LOUISA CATHERINE ADAMS, (Mrs. John Quincy Adams) Sixth Presiding Lady, 1825-1829.	117

Illustration Number		Page Number
141.	EMILY DONELSON, (Mrs. Andrew Jackson Donelson) Seventh Presiding Lady, 1829-1836. (She served in lieu of Rachel Donelson Jackson, wife of President Andrew Jackson.)	118
142.	SARAH YORKE JACKSON, (Mrs. Andrew Jackson, Jr.) Presiding Lady the last year of the Jackson Administration, 1837, and assistant to Mrs. Donelson, 1831-1836.	118
143.	ANGELICA VAN BUREN, (Mrs. Abraham Van Buren) Eighth Presiding Lady, 1839-1841.	119
144.	JUNE IRWIN FINDLAY, (Mrs. James Findlay) Ninth Presiding Lady, (in lieu of Anna Symmes Harrison, wife of President William Henry Harrison) 1841.	119
145.	LETITIA CHRISTIAN TYLER, (Mrs. John Tyler) Tenth Presiding Lady, 1841-1842.	120
146.	JULIA GARDINER TYLER, (Mrs. John Tyler) Later Presiding Lady of the Tenth Administration, 1844-1845.	120
147.	SARAH CHILDRESS POLK, (Mrs. James Knox Polk) Eleventh Presiding Lady, 1845-1849.	121
148.	COSTUME OF BETTY TAYLOR BLISS-DANDRIDGE, Twelfth Presiding Lady, 1849-1850. (She served in place of her mother, Margaret Smith Taylor, wife of President Zachary Taylor.	122
149.	ABIGAIL POWERS FILLMORE, (Mrs. Millard Fillmore) Thirteenth Presiding Lady, 1850-1853.	123
150.	JANE APPLETON PIERCE, (Mrs. Franklin Pierce) Fourteenth Presiding Lady, 1853-1857.	124
151.	HARRIET LANE JOHNSTON, (Mrs. Henry Eliot Johnston) Fifteenth Presiding Lady, (James Buchanan's Administration) 1857-1861.	125
152.	MARY TODD LINCOLN, (Mrs. Abraham Lincoln) Sixteenth Presiding Lady, 1861-1865.	126
153.	MARTHA JOHNSON PATTERSON, (Mrs. David T. Patterson) Seventeenth Presiding Lady, (Andrew Johnson's Administration) 1865-1869.	126
154.	JULIA DENT GRANT, (Mrs. Ulysses Simpson Grant) Eighteenth Presiding Lady, 1869-1877.	127
155.	LUCY WEBB HAYES, (Mrs. Rutherford B. Hayes) Nineteenth Presiding Lady, 1877-1881.	127
156.	LUCRETIA RUDOLPH GARFIELD, (Mrs. James A. Garfield) Twentieth Presiding Lady, 1881.	128

Illustration Number		Page Number
157.	MARY ARTHUR MC ELROY, (Mrs. John E. McElroy, Chester A. Arthur's Administration) Twenty-first Presiding Lady, 1881-1885.	129
158.	FRANCES FOLSOM CLEVELAND, (Mrs. Grover Cleveland) Twenty-second Presiding Lady, 1886-1889; 1893-1897. a: Souvenir Distributed When Baby Ruth Cleveland was born at the White House.	130
159.	CAROLINE SCOTT HARRISON, (Mrs. Benjamin Harrison) Twenty-third Presiding Lady, 1889-1892.	131
160.	MARY HARRISON McKEE, (Mrs. James Robert McKee) Presiding Lady on the Death of her Mother, Mrs. Benjamin Harrison, 1892-1893.	131
161.	IDA SAXTON McKINLEY, (Mrs. William McKinley) Twenty-fourth Presiding Lady, 1897-1901.	132
162.	EDITH KERMIT CAROW ROOSEVELT, (Mrs. Theodore Roosevelt) Twenty-fifth Presiding Lady, 1901-1909.	133
163.	HELEN HERRON TAFT, (Mrs. William H. Taft) Twenty-sixth Presiding Lady, 1909-1913.	134
164.	ELLEN AXON WILSON, (Mrs. Woodrow Wilson) Twenty-seventh Presiding Lady, 1913-1917.	135
165.	EDITH BOLLING WILSON, (Mrs. Woodrow Wilson) Twenty-eighth Presiding Lady, 1917-1921.	135
166.	FLORENCE KLING HARDING, (Mrs. Warren G. Harding) Twenty-ninth Presiding Lady, 1921-1923.	136
167.	GRACE GOODHUE COOLIDGE, (Mrs. Calvin Coolidge) Thirtieth Presiding Lady, 1923-1929.	136
168.	LOU HENRY HOOVER, (Mrs. Herbert Clark Hoover) Thirty-first Presiding Lady, 1929-1933.	137
169.	ANNA ELEANOR ROOSEVELT, (Mrs. Franklin Delano Roosevelt) Thirty-second Presiding Lady, 1933-1945.	138
170.	EVOLUTION OF THE SHOE. 1. Mediaeval. 2. Renaissance. 3. Soilaret (Henry VII). 4. Henry VIII. 5. Fourteenth Century Sandal. 6. Early British. 7. Pompeiian. 8. 1790-1810. 9. First Empire. 10. 1810-1860. 11. 1860 and Later.	141
171.	CALCEI. (a) CREPEDA. (b)	141
172.	EARLY GREEK. (a) 600-146 B. C. (b)	141
173.	SIXTH CENTURY SHOES.	141

Illustration Number		Page Number
174.	EIGHTEENTH CENTURY SHOES. a: Brocaded (1735). b: Clog (1735). c: White Satin (1800). d. Mans Shoe. e. Brocaded (1771).	143
175.	PRE-CIVIL WAR FOOTWEAR (1820-1860).	143
176.	POULAINE. (a) WOODEN CLOG POULAINE. (b) CHRISTENING POULAINE. (c)	143
177.	VENETIAN SHOES, SIXTEENTH TO EIGHTEENTH CENTURIES.	143
178.	RAT-TAILED SHOES.	143
179.	ANTIQUE PAPIÉR-MÂCHÉ-HEADED DOLLS. a: Miss Bridgewater. b: Miss Beacon.	145
180.	CELICIA, Brown-eyed China Head with Lower Lashes.	145
181.	VICTORIA, a Papiér-Mâché Head of the 1820's.	145
182.	MISS GOODYEAR, a Fine Early Hard Rubber Doll.	146
183.	LAVINIA, One of the Rarest of China Heads.	146
184.	JULIETTE, a China Head with Long Snood.	146
185.	HEATHER, a China Head with Feather Decorations in Hair.	146
186.	MRS. BUMBLEBOTTOM, a China Head with Spit-curls.	146
187.	ROSALINE, a Parian Bisque circa 1880.	147
188.	EVA, a China Head with Snood and Tassels.	147
189.	BETH, a China Head with Rose and Medallion Decorations.	147
190.	PRINCESS, Parian Bisque with Snood on Crown of Head.	147
191.	MISS VERYSMART, a Small China Head with the "Latest" Hairdo of 1868.	147
192.	Front View of No. 181.	147
193.	ELSIE, a Rare Parian Bisque with Molded Ruffled Blouse.	149
194.	PRINCESS JUNIOR, a Rare Parian Bisque with Wreath of Flowers.	149
195.	RUTH, a Parian Bisque with Molded Fancy Blouse.	149
196.	ELMIRA, a Rare China Head with Snood.	149
197.	GRACE, One of the Rarer Parian Bisques with Molded Necklace and Braided Coiffure.	149
198.	GENEVA, a Typical Parian Bisque of the 1880's.	149

Illustration Number		Page Number
199.	"LADY HAMILTON," a Rare Parian with Gainsborough Hat.	150
200.	RARE PAPIÉR-MÂCHÉ Belonging to Mrs. V. B. Dewitt of New Paltz, N. Y.	150
201.	CAROLINA, a Small China Head with Fancy Hairdo.	150
202.	STONE BISQUE from The Children's Museum, Jamaica Plain, Mass.	150
203.	FINE CHINA WITH INSET GLASS EYES, Property of Mrs. H. B. Plumb, North Hollywood, California.	150
204.	"JENNY LIND" OF FINE CHINA.	150
205.	PANSY, a Parian Bisque of 1880.	150
206.	ELIZABETH, a Large Blond Bisque, circa 1885.	150
207.	GEORGE, a Swivel-necked China Doll Sold during the Civil War.	151
208.	LADY BELLE, a Post Civil War Parian Bisque.	151
209.	ALICE, a Fine Quality Parian Bisque Doll.	152
210.	JAMES, a Companion Piece to Alice.	152
211.	MUSIC BOX DOLL Owned by Mrs. Joseph Mallon of Philadelphia, Pa.	153
212.	JACK, a Trick Doll.	153
213.	"JENNY LIND," a Doll Reproduced by Mrs. Emma C. Clear of Redondo Beach, California.	154
214.	"PRINCESS MARY AUGUSTA," Reproduced by Mrs. Clear.	154
215.	"MONA LISA," Reproduced by Mrs. Clear.	155
216.	"AUGUSTA VICTORIA," Reproduced by Mrs. Clear.	155
217.	"LITTLE KATE GREENAWAY," Reproduced by Mrs. Clear.	155
218.	"CLAUDIA," Blond Bisque Reproduced by Mrs. Clear.	155
219.	"PARTHENIA," Parian Reproduced by Mrs. Clear.	155
220.	"SIR GALAHAD," Reproduced by Mrs. Clear.	156
221.	"GIBSON GIRL," Reproduced by Mrs. Clear.	156
222.	"SNOOTY," Reproduced by Mrs. Clear.	156
223.	"THE BLUE SCARF DOLL," Reproduced by Mrs. Clear.	156
224.	"BARBARY COAST GENT," Reproduced by Mrs. Clear (with mustachios added.)	156

Illustration Number		Page Number
225.	"YOUNG VICTORIA," Reproduced by Mrs. Clear.	156
226.	"ELIZABETH PARIAN," Reproduced by Mrs. Clear.	157
227.	"DOLLY MADISON," Reproduced by Mrs. Clear.	157
228.	"SPILL CURLS," Reproduced by Mrs. Clear.	157
229.	"CURLY TOP," Reproduced by Mrs. Clear.	158

IN APPRECIATION

I wish to acknowledge with grateful thanks the cooperation given me by Miss Margaret W. Brown and Mrs. Catherine Manning of the Smithsonian Institution; and Mrs. J. Cleves Symmes of Atlanta, Georgia, in my search for photographs of the White House hostesses on which to base my sketches of those ladies. Also to Mrs. Florence G. Martin of the Library of Congress for the help she has given me in locating costumes of the past.

CLARA HALLARD FAWCETT

The Author Conceives A Doll
To Symbolize the Subject of her Book.

ON MAKING, MENDING AND DRESSING DOLLS

Chapter I

A Simple Doll for a Small Child— The Rag Doll

HOW far back the rag doll goes into the dim periods of history is anyone's guess. Probably the first doll of this kind came into being shortly after the invention of cloth, for we know that as soon as a country became civilized, and all hands were not required to labor from sunup to sundown for a mere existence, dolls were fashioned from available material.

Throughout recorded history rag dolls have had an affectionate place in the heart of womankind. When the super de luxe French doll, in all her gorgeous trappings, queened over the ordinary nursery variety, verses by the ream were written about the old rag doll versus the new and glamorous French creation popular from fifty to a hundred years ago. Hundreds of patterns for rag dolls in the nineteenth and twentieth century records of the Patent Office, Washington, D. C., attest to the popularity of cloth, and patterns for this childhood favorite appeared frequently in magazines and newspapers of the long past just as they do in the present. "No family of dolls is complete," says "The Delineator"—Fashions for December, 1882, "that does not include a real rag doll, which will bear any amount of hugging without losing color or having its joints put out of place."

The simplest of all to make is the stocking doll. Most of those we see are not especially attractive, but they can be made so by selecting a sock of fine quality and appropriate size, taking pains with the features and stuffing, and adding color.

Choose a three-quarters' length sock in colors, flesh, white or tan; brown or black if you wish to make a colored baby. Turn the sock inside out, and it will be ready for stitching when you cut around the foot, as shown in illustration. Do not cut into the heel, as this forms the rump of the doll. The two halves of the foot make the legs. Sew together a and b, reverse and stuff to just above the cuff line. Pack extra stuffing where it is advisable to round out, such as the feet. Tie tightly directly above the stuffing with strong thread. The loose cuff forms the cap of the doll. Pull it down over the face. Now fold upward to make the brim of the cap. The neckline is indicated by a running stitch. Use the foot of the second sock to make arms. (See illustration 1-c)

Make tassels for cap, shoulder and hands, by wrapping wool around a card (1-d) twice the length you wish your tassel to be. Pull gently off the card, so as

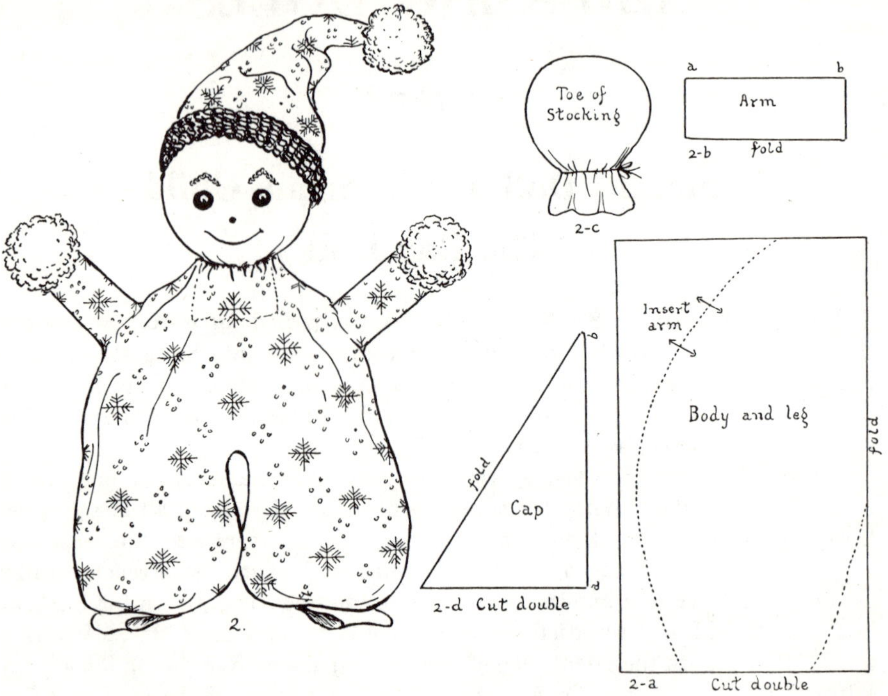

On Making, Mending and Dressing Dolls

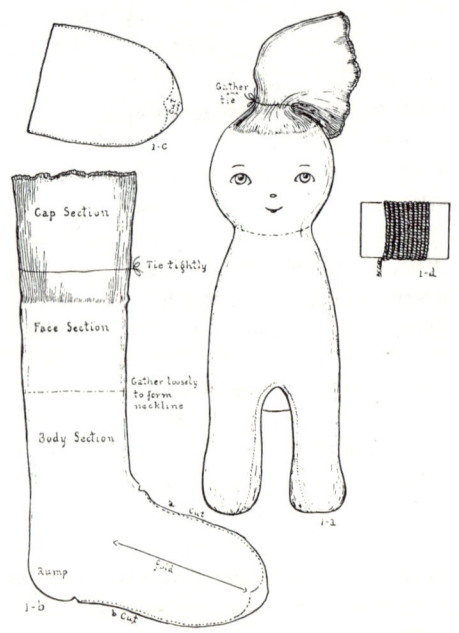

1. Sock Doll.

   1-a to 1-d—Pattern for Making Sock Doll.

2. Bean Bag Doll.

   2-a to 2-d—Patterns for Making and Dressing Bean Bag Doll.

not to disturb the winding. Tie together tightly in the center, round out the edges and trim with scissors. Soft, fluffy wool, wound thickly around the card, makes a plump, pretty tassel.

This doll is a favorite for groups (such as the Camp Fire Girls and Girl Scouts) to make for small children in hospitals and foundling homes. It is easily and quickly made and appeals especially to the youngest set.

Another simple doll for children, and one which provides active fun for them, is Benjamin, the Bean Bag Doll. He can be tossed about from one to the other, and if he falls it doesn't matter, for he lands on his feet smiling graciously all the while. His anatomy from the neck down is also his costume.

The body (arms excepted) is made in two pieces, each cut double as in diagram 2-a, which shows half of the front and back portions, with the fold between the neckline and the crotch of the pants-leg. Sew (always on wrong side of cloth, then reverse) front and back halves together where dotted lines show in the illustration, leaving open the portion between the double arrows for the insertion of arms. Arms are straight tubes of cloth. Diagram 2-b shows half of one arm. Stitch together between points a and b. The head may be the toe of a stocking or sock stuffed with cotton batting or similar material and tied with a string at the neckline. This is inserted into the shirred neckline of the costume. Features may be painted or embroidered. Before placing the head into position, fill the pants-legs with beans to the crotch.

Measure the head carefully before cutting pattern (2-d) for the cap, leaving space for seams. Tassels may be hand-made as described in the directions for making a sock doll, or they may be tassels cut from drapery fringe purchased by the yard at any department store. Hand-made tassels are usually more colorful and attractive, and offer a wider range as to size.

Another doll easily made is Anne. (See illustration No. 3) Clubs cooperating in the making of dolls to give away at Christmas time will welcome this pattern. If one will master the simple art of block printing, Anne's face may be printed by the dozens. Use tracing paper and carbon to transfer the face (3-b) onto a piece of plain battleship linoleum. With a small pocket knife, carving tools or an "Exacto" blade cut away all but the features, leaving the latter in relief. Use oil paint the consistency of thick cream to make the transfer, and provide yourself with a padded board (an ironing board will do) over which to spread the muslin to be printed. Dampen the latter before placing the painted features face down on the cloth. In painting the surface, use a flat bristle brush. Press down with the hands for a few seconds before lifting the block from the cloth. If edges are blurred, your paint is too thick. A little practice helps in securing satisfactory results.

The pattern for Anne is so simple that words hardly are necessary to describe the making of her. Cut all sections double and sew on dotted lines on wrong side of cloth, then reverse. An opening should be left at the bottom of the body and the top of the arms and legs through which to place the stuffing. A dart at center neckline rounds out the face. Another at the top of the head helps in this respect.

If you are using a separate piece for a block-printed face, leave plenty of cloth around it so that the edges, when placed in position, will overlap at the back of the head, where it may be sewn and the edges covered with hair. The advantage of a face which may be removed for cleaning is obvious.

Anne's clothes are as simple to make as the doll herself. Diagram 3-e shows one-half of one side of the pants (the other side is folded under.) Cut two. The two pant-sides should be sewn together, front and back, between the crotch and the waist before the legs are sewn.

Diagram 3-c shows one-half of the front of the waist (the other side is folded under.) Cut two, making the second one, the back, a little wider than

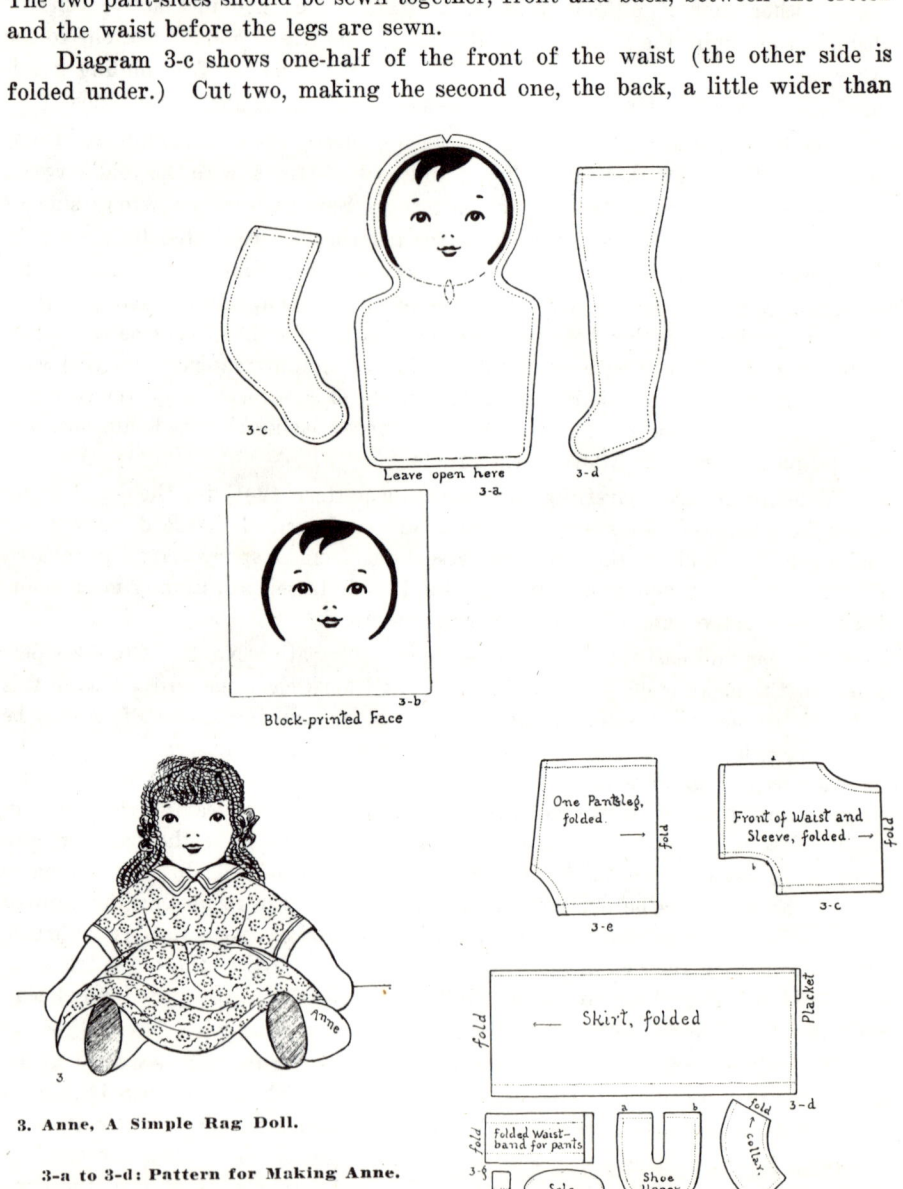

3. Anne, A Simple Rag Doll.

3-a to 3-d: Pattern for Making Anne.

3-e to 3-i: Patterns for Clothing Anne.

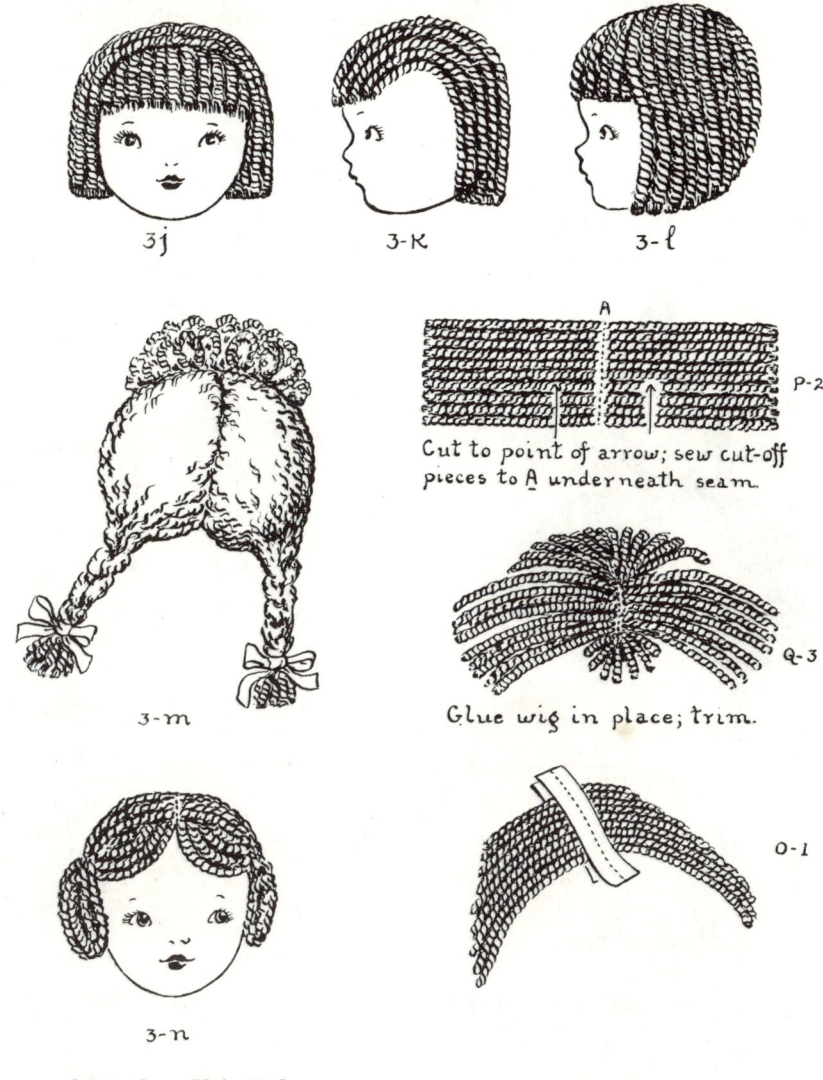

3-j to 3-n: Hair Styles.   O-1 to Q-3: Making a Wig.

the front. Slit down the middle of the back to make the opening. The excess width is for the hem. Sew the two sides together at a and b. The skirt is a straight piece, as shown. It should be shirred to the waist. The band (3-g) is optional.

Fold collar and cut as indicated (3-f) and sew to neckline.

Shoes may be made of thin felt. The upper (3-h) is sewn together at a and b, the lower rim stitched to the rim of the sole (3-i.) Bow for the shoe is optional.

The accompanying sketches show how to make and arrange a yarn wig for Anne and similar dolls.

Susie; Rag Doll No. 4, seems to have been a favorite about 1900. She turns up occasionally in thrift shops or antique stores. Clothes that accompany her indicate approximately the period. The writer has been able to find three such dolls. All have the same printed features with eyes and lips so beautifully finished that they seem hand-painted. The nose, eyes and brows are delicately

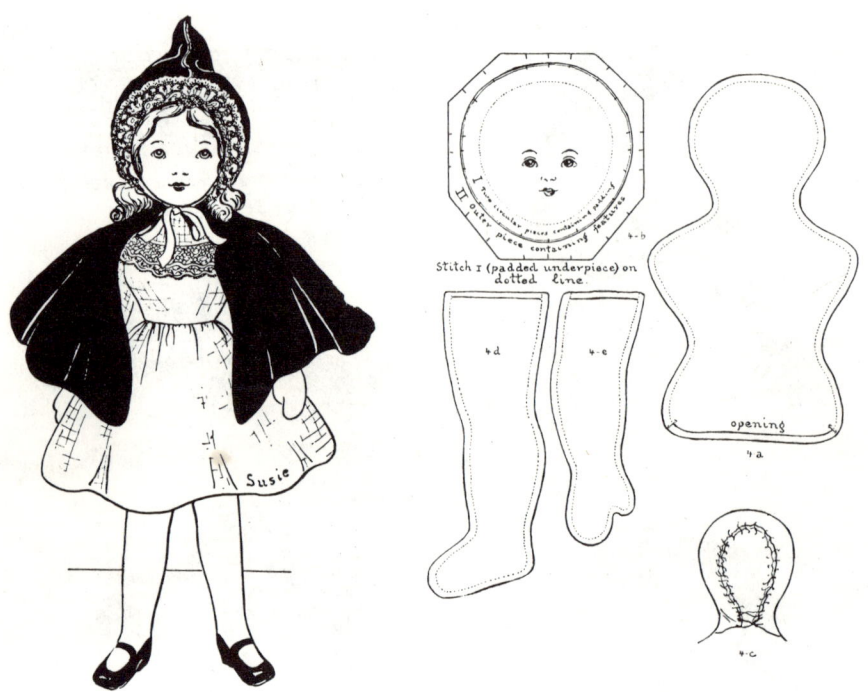

Ill. 4. Susie, A Rag Doll Circa 1900; at right (4a-4d) is shown Pattern for Making Susie.

outlined, and all are well-made, although the material and hair differ. Susie (see illustration) has beautiful flaxen locks, and her body is of fine muslin. She came equipped with a splendid wardrobe.

The trunk and head are in two pieces; sketch 4-a should be cut double to form the front and back. Use unbleached muslin or similar material. Stitch around the edge, leaving a space at the bottom for stuffing. Lamb's wool is always the best for this purpose, as it is resilient, yet firm and never lumpy. Kapok is the next best, and cotton batting third. Old pieces of soft cloth or fragments of stockings will answer the purpose, however. One can always manage to make a rag doll with material on hand in the average household.

A Simple Doll for a Small Child—The Rag Doll

The face is rounded out by an extra pad (4-b). Place padding between two circles of cheesecloth (See No. I inside rectangle). The dotted line represents the stitches circling the padding. The outer octangular piece of cloth marked II contains the features. This piece should be placed over the head and sewn to the back of the head as in sketch 4-c. Cuts indicated in the edge of the cloth are for greater facility in smoothing the edges to the head of the doll.

The leg (4-d) and arm (4-e) are each cut double and stitched as indicated, with the usual opening at the top for stuffing. 4-f is the completed doll.

4-f: Susie, Completed.

A. Dress for Susie.
B. Bonnet for Susie.

The little gingham dress and bonnet A and B accompanied Susie, and are fine examples of the period. Diagram C shows the pattern for the above dress. No. 1 shows half the yoke. Cut folded as indicated.

No. 2 shows half the lower part of the waist. This should be shirred as indicated by the wavy line, the upper part stitched to the lower part of the yoke, the lower part to the waist band.

No. 3 shows half the back. Turn under and hem at dot-and-dash line. No. 5 shows half the shoulder tab, No. 6 the belt, and No. 7 half the cuff. The sleeve (No. 4) may be shortened or lengthened as desired. The oblong embracing the rest of the pattern parts is half the skirt. Fold and cut. Trim with lace and braid.

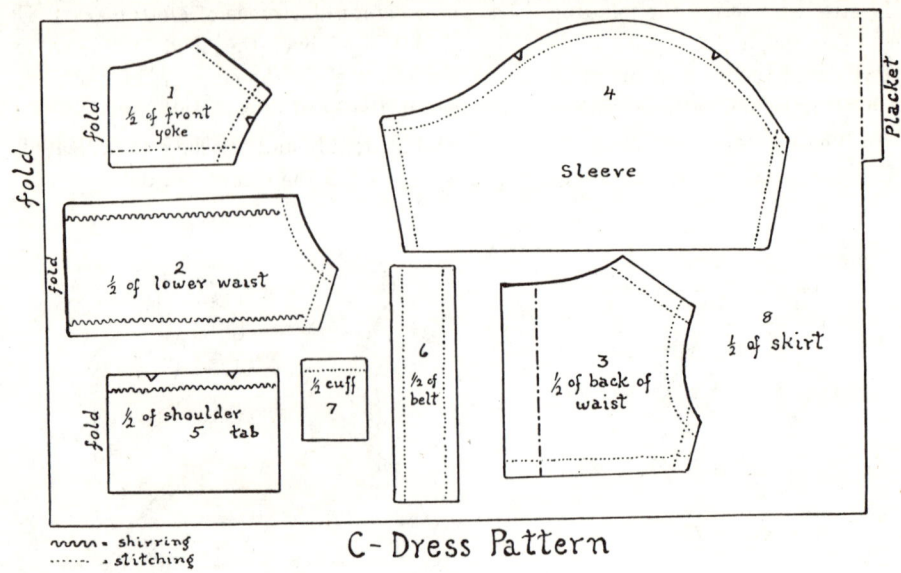

C-Dress Pattern

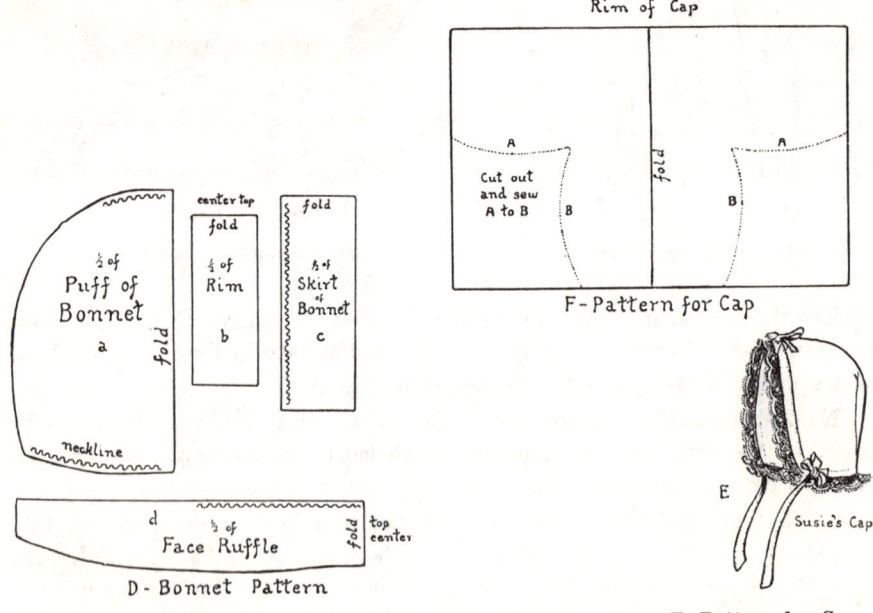

D-Bonnet Pattern

F-Pattern for Cap

Susie's Cap

C. Susie's Dress Pattern. D. Bonnet Pattern. E. Susie's Cap. F. Pattern for Cap.

Diagram D is for the gingham bonnet. Cut two of a; fold and cut b, c and d; d is for the ruffle around the face, and the fold indicates the top center. Shirr the puff of the bonnet as indicated at the top, where it is sewn to the top center of the rim or band of the bonnet. Shirr also at the neck (center back) where it is sewn to the skirt of the bonnet. The face ruffle is shirred only at top center. Ties for the bonnet may be of self material or of ribbon. Trim with lace edging.

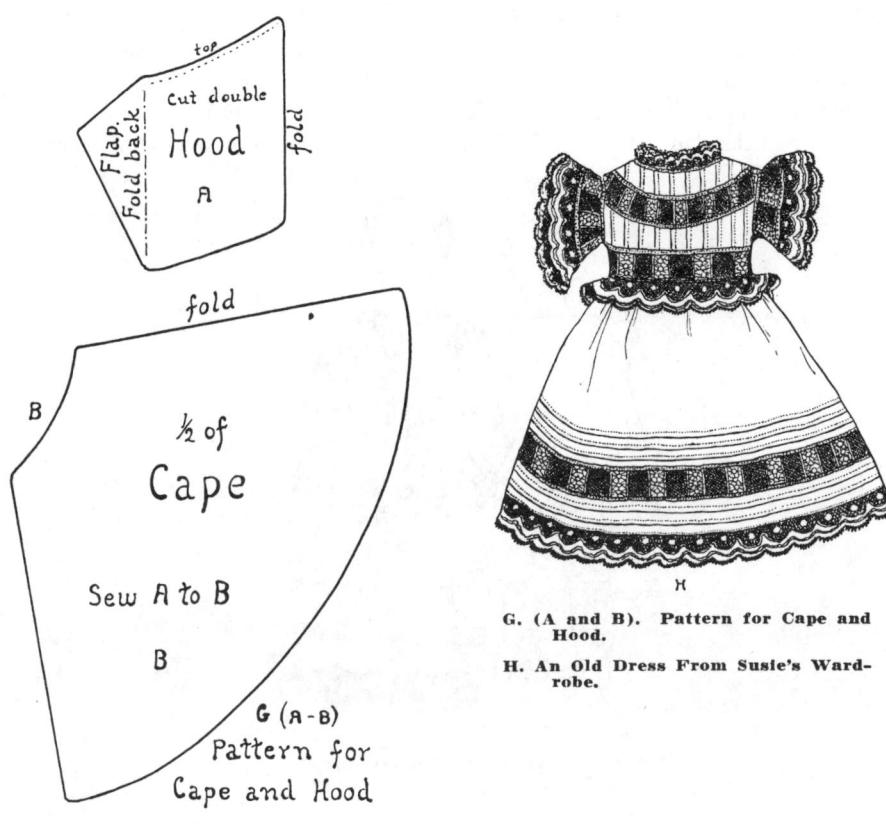

G. (A and B). Pattern for Cape and Hood.

H. An Old Dress From Susie's Wardrobe.

Susie's "Red Riding Hood" outfit is most attractive. E is the white lace-trimmed cap which came underneath the hood. F is the pattern for the cap. Cut as indicated, and sew A to B on either side. Ribbon bows and ties add charm. G is the hood. Fold and cut. Sew the top together as far as the flap, which folds back at dot-and-dash line. Fold the cape, G, and cut. Sew A to B and hem the edges. Fasten with ties.

H is Susie's party dress. The pattern for Anne's dress may be used for this by substituting a lace ruffle for the kimono sleeves.

Chapter II

Cloth Dolls for Collectors

GENEVIEVE (No. 5) is really a collector's item, or would be if in better condition. She was found in an old battered trunk, rusty on its hinges and smelling of musty years under musty attic beams. Aunt Nellie had loved and played with Genevieve nearly all of her active childhood. Finally, battered and worn as the doll was with the struggle against Nellie's too-great affection, she had been laid to sleep along with treasured trinkets of an age only occasionally brought to mind as Nellie lived through adolescence and maturity, and at last entered upon that "greatest of all adventures." As the lid of Genevieve's trunk

5. Genevieve, a 19th Century Rag Doll.

was lifted, she gave the same happy unconcerned smile that she had bestowed upon Nellie nearly eighty years before.

Nellie must have loved Genevieve to have treasured her remains, for the latter were found in a condition unfit to serve any purpose but as a pattern for a new doll. And so arose, like the phoenix of old, a new and fresher Genevieve, "most beautiful to see." Dear Genevieve, when ripped apart, destuffed and laid out flat, looked twice as wide as previously. One would scarcely believe that in the taking up of darts, and rounding out of the completed twenty-inch doll, she would lose in waist measure exactly one-half, and more than that at the neck. You will find that when completed your Genevieve will have tall, slender, lady-like proportions, and, unless you vary the pattern to suit your own ideas of what a doll should look like, she will have the long, drooping shoulders popular in the 1870's and earlier.

Before cutting pattern 5-a, the head and trunk of Genevieve, trace the features and hair onto the head. Higgins' American inks (brown for the hair, brows, eyelashes and nostrils, blue for the eyes and red for the lips) are recommended for this purpose if you wish to make your doll as nearly like the original as possible. 5-b represents one-half the back of the doll. Cut double and sew together straight down the center back and head. Before sewing back to front, join the notches at top and neck of 5-a, and at the top of 5-b. Remember that the bottom of the trunk should be left open until the stuffing is inserted. The

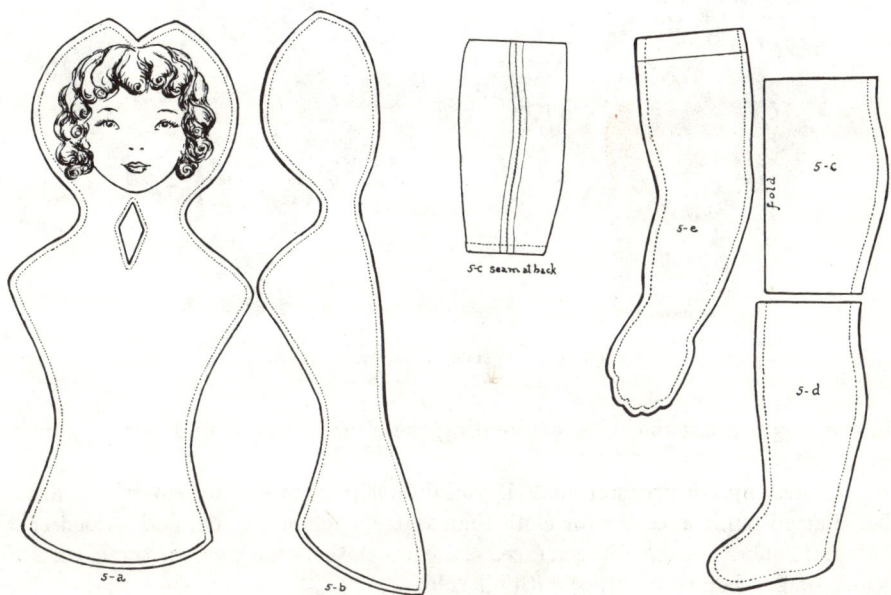

5-a - 5-d: Pattern for Making Genevieve.

bottom part is longer at the back, but when this is brought forward and sewn to the front, it forms the rump of the doll.

Pack firmly with any desired stuffing, although sawdust is best for a doll of this size. Few persons who are beginners realize the value of careful stuffing—it can make or mar a hand-made doll. Factories have machines for this purpose and are able to make solid stuffing. That done by hand is apt to be too loose unless the doll-maker has had practice.

Fold and cut double the upper leg portion (5-c). At this time, sew only at dotted line. Now press flat, so that the seam is in the center of the back (5-e). Stitch the lower edge in this position. Reverse, as always, so that the seam is inside, stuff and sew up the top.

5-d, the lower leg part, is cut in two pieces for each leg and foot. Stitch together, leaving the upper end open so that the leg may be reversed and stuffed.

Proceed in the same manner with the arm. Stuffing in the arm should not reach quite to the top, as it is always well to turn in about half an inch of the cloth before attaching it to the shoulder.

If you prefer to have Genevieve as a child rather than a tall young lady, vary the pattern to suit the child figure—square the shoulders, make only a tiny tuck at the throat, and shorten the body and limbs. The rather large dart shown

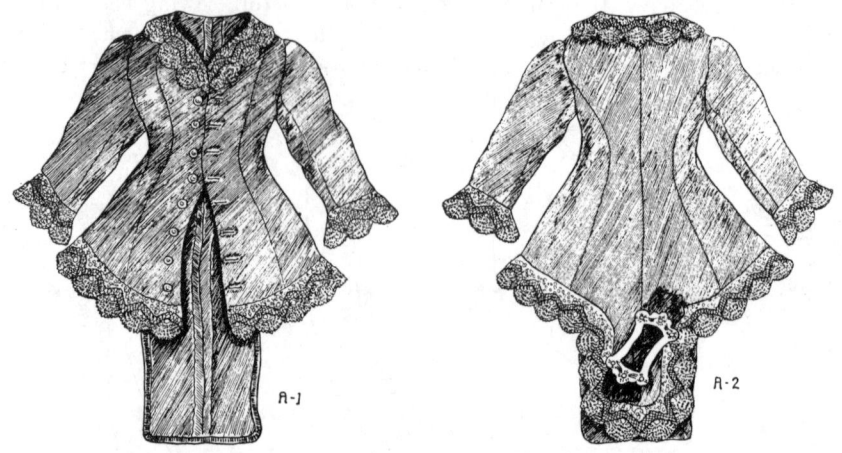

A-1 - A-2: A Basque for Genevieve.

in the diagram has the effect of pointing the chin and making a more "grown-up" face.

In making features and hair, if you do not plan to use ink entirely, remember that oil paint is better for cloth than water color or crayon, and a good coat of paint makes a cleanable surface. If your cloth is too porous, try a coat of white shellac before painting with oil colors.

Genevieve's beautiful original basque dress (sketches A-1, A-2, A-3) is of taupe velvet with taffeta ruffles in a lighter shade. The neck, sleeves and bottom of the basque are trimmed with fine hand-made crocheted lace, and on the coat-tail is a metal buckle fastening a bow of dark taupe ribbon.

Both front and back of the bodice are cut in four pieces. Cut two of each in the diagram and sew together as indicated by darts. The center front is left open. Diagrams 5 and 6 represent the two parts of each sleeve. These should be cut double, one set for each sleeve, and sewn together as indicated by the darts.

No. 1 "A Skirt for Genevieve" should be cut double on a fold, as indicated. It represents the front gore. No. 2 (cut double) represents the two side gores, and No. 3 (cut double) the two back gores. No. 4 is half the belt and should be cut double on a fold. Dotted lines show seams to be stitched, and the notches where the two parts in each case are fitted together. Ruffles may be added as desired.

Except for heels, which are difficult to make, the shoe, No. 10, is typical of the late nineteenth century. Cut double on a fold, as indicated in a and b, and stitch toe to upper part of boot. The sole (No. 9) will require patience in at-

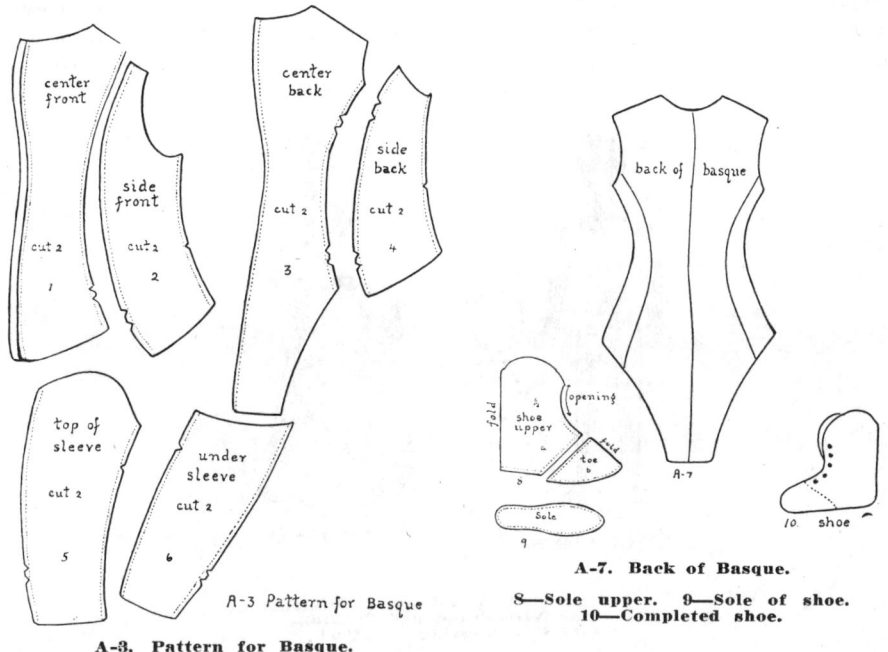

A-3. Pattern for Basque.

A-7. Back of Basque.
8—Sole upper. 9—Sole of shoe.
10—Completed shoe.

C—A Skirt for Genevieve.
(See Ill. #11 for Pattern)

taching to the upper. If you have no small old buttons, use tiny round paper fasteners. An old kid glove is just the thing for making dolls' shoes. Genevieve's old shoe was taken apart in order to make this pattern.

Winifred (No. 6) is built over a wire armature, a favorite method of many doll makers, especially those who wish the nine- or ten-inch size, or the even smaller doll-house doll. The figure may be bent in any direction; it can sit, walk, stand, bend over a wee cook-stove, and do all the active things connected with keeping house or working or playing out of doors. The tiny wire-framed doll can be made of odds and ends found about any household, and accessories for it are abundant. A thimble makes a dapper "stove-pipe" hat, a painted aspirin

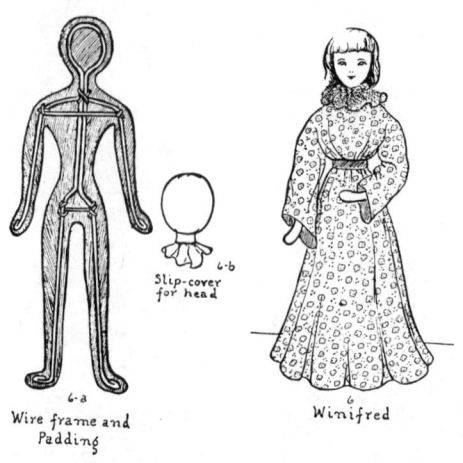

Winifred, A Wire-Framed Doll.
6-a: Wire Frame and Padding.
6-b: Slip Covering for Head.

box a perfect suit-case, etc. And one has only to make a tour of house, garden or woodlot to find countless suggestions for furnishing the small fellow with equipment for any "employment" he has, whether as soldier, sailor, butcher, baker, gardener, plowman or fisherman. Your findings will surprise and delight you.

In making the doll, be careful of proportion. Human proportions of the ideal six-footer (eight heads high) are fine in a painting, or in picturing a tall hero, but for the average small figure, seven or even six heads high, seems more natural. Arms should reach half way from the shoulder to the foot.

For the ten-inch doll, ordinary baling wire, which may be bought at any hardware store, is satisfactory. For a doll-house doll, wire about half this width will do. Wire which comes around milk bottle tops in some sections of the country has many purposes. It may be used for fastening armature wires in place; and for tiny doll-house dolls, it can be used (double-twisted) for the armature itself.

Sketch 6-a shows one way to make a wire frame, and the thickness of the padding needed. Other ways of making the armature will suggest themselves as you go along. Small pliers are necessary to bend into shape the wire of the larger doll, especially at the hands and feet. Reinforce the bailing wire at chest and hips, as shown in diagram.

When the armature is made, cut strips of cloth from old stockings or discarded cotton jersey undershirts. Wrap tightly around the framework of the doll, tacking together with needle and thread where necessary. With further wrappings, build out to the desired shape, using extra padding at head, chest and seat. The head should be finished by a slip-covering, and tightened at the neck with adhesive tape. Covering for the head might be the toe of a small stocking for the larger doll, a glove finger tip for a tiny one. Hair may be made of silk stocking ravelings, feather tips, clippings of fur, yarn or what-have-you. Winifred's "crowning glory" was fashioned from the soft silken hair which grew on the end of a poodle dog's tail. Tinkie, the generous donor, gladly contributed a bit of his personality for so noble a cause.

Persons particularly interested in this type of doll would do well to study Nina R. Jordan's "American Dolls In Uniform," which gives detailed information about its construction.

Chapter III

On Carving and Modeling Dolls

CLAIRE FAWCETT, daughter of the writer, tells the story of how to carve a doll. She has made hundreds, from tiny figures an inch high to jointed "play" dolls of twenty inches or more. For tools she relies mostly upon an ordinary pen knife or "Exacto" blade, but in carving the hair, finds carving tools (see illustration) a help. The drill and awl shown in the sketch are used for drilling holes where the limbs are joined to the body. Wood is purchased from a lumber yard, often salvaged from a scrap heap at no cost. Preferences are white pine, cypress, gumwood, white wood, all easy to carve; but for a small

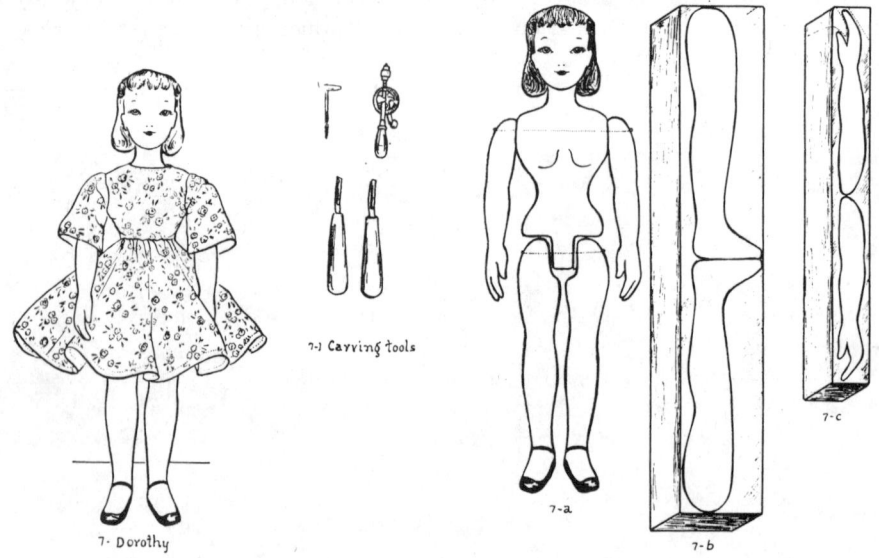

7. Dorothy, A Doll Carved by Claire Fawcett. 7-1. Carving Tools.
7-a, 7-c: Parts of Carved Doll.

hand with separate fingers one would have to use a hard wood like cherry; otherwise the fingers would chip off on the slightest provocation.

The work seems easy to Claire—"It's like peeling potatoes" she says. However, it is not easy for the beginner; it does require practice. In carving, many small things have to be taken into consideration. For instance, one does not start to carve a little doll on just the right sized wood to contain the little figure. One must leave a "handle" to hold on to while carving. Choice of wood is important. Be careful that the wood you choose has no knots or cracks and is fine-grained. Sometimes the cracks are not apparent until one looks at the end and sees them spiralling out from the center.

Claire warns that every attempt at carving goes through what she calls "a discouraging stage." Even today, after years of practice, she always comes to a point in her carving where she thinks "Heavens, this thing will never look like anything!" But it always turns out satisfactorily.

First make a rough sketch of what you want to carve. "You will find your figure changing as you go along" warns Claire, "but the sketch will help in the matter of proportions. Start with the head."

When the carving is finished, smooth with fine sandpaper or emery cloth. A stiff emery paper file is just the thing to take care of edges, such as the ruff of a clown. Start with something simple. Elaborate carving is not necessary for a doll. A face with good proportions and simple lines can be made as lovely as you wish with paint properly applied. If the doll is tiny, use pen and India ink for lashes and eyebrows. Leave a highlight in the pupil of each eye and on the mouth. If you will study the sketches, you will find that the lips do not meet on one side. This gives a better effect than it otherwise would. Study your own face in the mirror for proportions.

In carving arms and legs for Dorothy (Doll No. 7) a piece of wood the length of the two legs placed foot to foot, and another piece the length of the two arms placed end to end, was used. (See illustration.) This facilitates carving. Saw off the ends of the stick of wood on which the hands and arms are sketched before starting to carve. And it will help in carving the legs if you will first eliminate the rather large piece of unnecessary wood between points 1 and 2.

Dotted lines in Figure 7-a between the shoulders and hips show where the drill has been used to make a passage way for wires to hold the movable limbs in place.

Dorothy's corn-colored hair is shaded, and there is a small red bow painted on either side of the head. Mary Jane slippers are also painted on.

If you will make a small waist for your "growing girl" doll, she will look more attractive when dressed. In making a pattern for this doll, place paper over the torso and sketch an outline, making sure that you allow for seams. Sleeves are straight pieces of cloth, rounded a bit at the top. The plain skirt is slightly gored.

Su-su (No. 8) and Silly the clown (No. 9) are made a little differently. In each case, head, shoulders, forearms and legs to the knee are of wood; the rest of the body is of cloth stuffed with sawdust. This method makes a hugable doll. Notice the ridge in the hand and foot (No. 9). This facilitates fastening the cloth to the wooden parts of the doll.

Silly's clothes 9-a are very simple to make. A represents half the smock, which should be cut double on the fold for both front and back, if you wish to make it all in one piece. However, if it is to be a coat effect, like the sketch, cut the front halves separately, making each side marked "fold" a little wider to take care of the hem.

B, cut double on the fold, represents one pants-leg. Stitch each side to the placket line. Sew the two pants-legs together at the crotch. C represents one-half the ruff, and should also be cut double on the fold. The pants may be either bell-shaped or gathered with a ruffle at the ankle. If made of contrasting materials, and trimmed with rickrack braid, as in the sketch, it will make an effective outfit. Silly's costume is red and white, the white part trimmed

8. Su-su. A Doll with Carved Head, Arms and Legs, Stuffed Body, by Claire Fawcett.

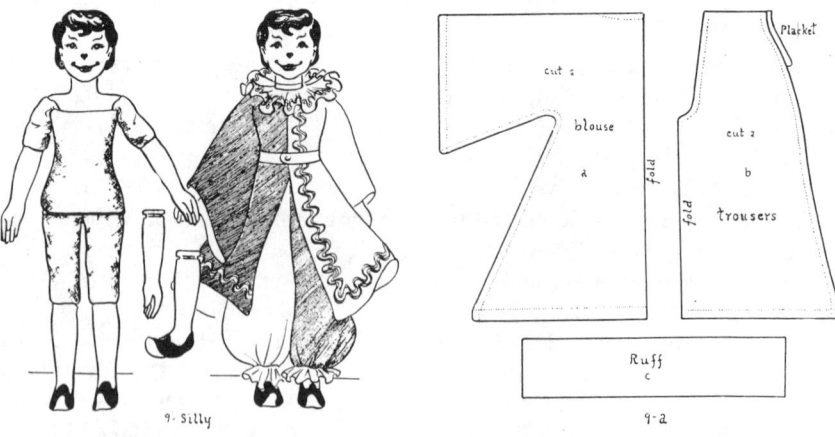

9. Silly, the Clown, by Claire Fawcett.   9-a. Pattern for Silly's Costume.

with red braid, and the red part trimmed with white braid. His shoes are red with yellow soles to add color. Altogether, he is an attractive young fellow with his wee red-heart nose and wide grin.

From carving single figures, Claire tried sets with scenic backgrounds done in soft shades of water color which did not clash with the more brilliant oil-painted figures. For years the Christmas centerpieces in the Fawcett menage were Claire's creations. One year it was the Nativity scene, another St. Francis and all the little animals and birds he was supposed to feed; still another, a family gathered around the Christmas tree and receiving guests laden with packages; another scene represented the hearthfire in a fifteenth century mansion with carolers mingled with the family, and musicians playing on old-fashioned instruments. The most spectacular scene is a circus wedding procession reaching all the way around a large table; and the most difficult of all to make is a merry-go-round which really goes around most merrily. Clowns and Santa Clauses and "play" dolls abound. Collectors who visit like the ones with swinging arms and legs. There is something solid and substantial about a wooden doll. The passing years may fade the paint, but in the fading a softer, more attractive shade often develops. And a wooden doll, with ordinary care, will survive the centuries—something to think about when one has labored long and earnestly on a thing of beauty, which, as the poet says, should be "a joy forever."

Some persons find it easier to model than to carve. The love of modeling is in the heart of humankind whether or not life and its various experiences have conspired to bring out this special talent. Primitive man possessed it; it meant better living when, after the discovery of fire and its capacity to change the flavor of food, he needed vessels in which to cook it, as well as to carry water. Necessity may be the mother of invention, but it is also the grandmother of a love of art for art's sake. Otherwise, we would not have the beautiful figures, statuary and vases that have adorned our homes and public buildings long since the actual need for the purely useful had been satisfied. No one who has done any modeling will forget the thrill experienced over the first finished piece. The writer's earliest effort was intended to be a mug, but turned out a sugar bowl. However, it was an attractive sugar bowl, and formed the nucleus of what was later to be a bride's only dishes.

From modeling dishes to modeling dolls is just a step, and yet it was a long time before the writer gained the confidence to try, thus missing a lot of fun she might have had at an earlier period in life.

Sketch No. 10 pictures George, a Colonial gentleman of quality. His head is modeled by hand of the same material described in the mending of "Grandmother's doll," Chapter IV. The stick which forms the armature for his head reaches down into his sawdust body below the waistline. Hands are of carved wood and hair of fine raw silk. His dark blue velvet coat is trimmed with lace at the cuffs, which matches his stock. Knee breeches of cream colored velvet make a good contrast to the coat. George has a brocaded silk waistcoat (made from the inside of a discarded tie) buttoned with tiny round brass paper fasteners, and his square-toed kid shoes once enveloped a ladies' hand as gloves. Very little did a certain child dream as she discarded the tinfoil from a chocolate bar

10. George, A Doll Modelled by Clara Hallard Fawcett.

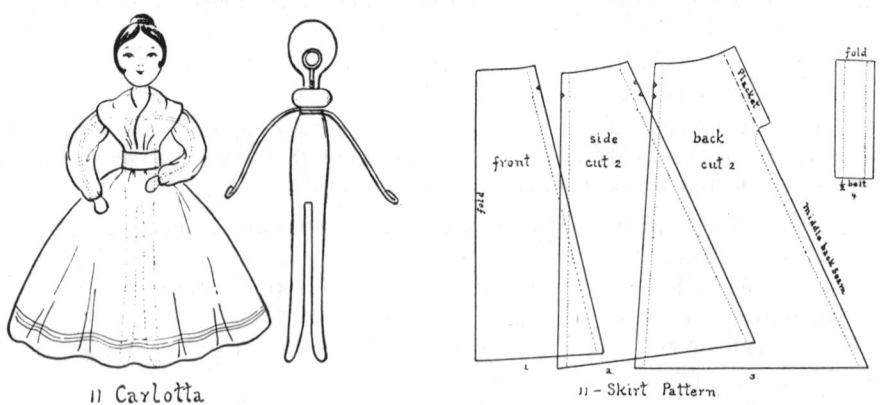

11. Carlotta, the Clothespin Lady. At right, pattern for her skirt.

that one day that same tinfoil would appear as buckles on the shoes of an eighteenth century gentleman.

Carlotta, the clothespin lady, (No. 11) has a head built up over a screw eye placed in the top of a clothespin. Wire arms fastened around the neck of the clothespin should be padded with Scot towelling, and the shoulders built out in the same way. Her head may be made of white modeling clay, or, if a very light weight is desired, of papiér mâché powder mixed with paste. Her hairdo is modeled and painted. These make interesting place cards at Doll Club parties. Each might wear a little white apron bearing the name of the guest. If well made, they are readily sold at fairs.

For those who find modeling difficult, the cast method of making a doll head from a commercial one might be tried. Some like to use the cast method for reproducing an original head. If this fits your case, you will find that modeling clay over a stick placed upright in a block of wood (diagram a) will be convenient. If you have not the tool for drilling a sufficiently large hole in the block to contain the stick, your hardware store man will be glad to oblige.

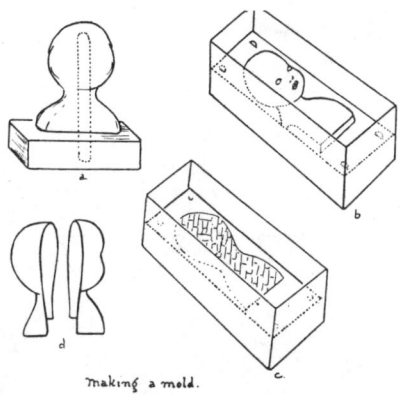

making a mold.

a-d: Making a Mold.

After the head is modeled to your satisfaction, find a cardboard box in which it will fit with not too much space around the edges. Fill half way to the top of the reclining figure, which previously has been thoroughly greased, with liquid plaster of Paris about the consistency of thick cream. When the plaster has settled enough, place a marble at each corner. Half of each marble should protrude from the plaster. As soon as the latter is hard, grease the whole surface and fill the box so that it completely covers the bust. The idea is to get two complete molds divided exactly from the center of each shoulder around the head. Greasing the head and the division in plaster between the two parts enables you to take it out of the mold when the plaster has hardened. The marbles act as locks.

Plaster of Paris takes about half an hour to "set." During this time it will become warm. In an hour or so, when it cools off, the plaster is hard and you are ready to peel away the cardboard box, pry open the two halves of the mold (use the flat of a knife blade) and take out the head. You should have a neat impression ready to receive the papiér mâché. (See diagram c.)

Cut or tear little pieces of Scot towelling and paste, one overlapping the other, into each impression, until the latter is covered, making sure that you have first greased the impression. Make five or six layers, then allow to harden before taking from the mold. Trim the edges (diagram d), and paste the two sides together with an extra strip of paper or cheesecloth. Now the head is ready to be painted. Papiér mâché will take either oil or water colors, but if you use the latter, finish with white shellac; otherwise it will soil too readily.

Whether you carve, model by hand or use the cast system of making doll parts, your work will become more and more interesting as you go along, for with practice come ease of performance and better results.

Chapter IV

On Mending Dolls Old and New

JEAN was a new doll—well, almost new. Elsie, the small owner, had had the inexpressible joy of mothering Jean for nearly three months—and then it happened. Brother Johnie, whose laudable ambition was to become a famous surgeon, decided that Jean had a poisoned foot and that it must come off. His ideas on the subject of amputation at the time were a bit crude. When his toy saw wouldn't work fast enough, he used a hammer most effectively, for after one well directed blow, a shattered doll's foot lay beside the jagged edge of a leg, and a piercing shriek from Elsie brought Mother to the spot in less time than it takes to tell it. To quote Mark Twain, "Let us draw the curtain of charity over the scene which followed."

12. Jean—Before and After.

Elsie was inconsolable. But Mother finally convinced her that she herself would play doctor, a good doctor, and promised that Jean would have a new foot. She hadn't "read up" on doll mending for nothing. With three heaping tablespoonfulls of papiér maché powder, purchased at an arts and crafts shop, and one tablespoonful of wallpaper paste, well kneaded together with the help of the flat of a flexible table knife, she made a plastic which had the necessary adhesive qualities, and also could be modeled into the shape of a foot.

Elsie watched the process with a great deal of interest. "But you must let the foot dry for a week over the slow heat of a radiator," said Mother, "and then we will paint it with doll enamel which I also shall mix myself."

That afternoon Mother purchased for fifteen cents at the five-and-ten-cent store, one small can of white enamel, and, at the art store, a tube each of orange and red paint. The white enamel was tinted with a speck of orange, and this alone would have matched the color of some of Elsie's dolls, but Jean needed the tiniest speck of red added to blend with her rosier complexion. Mother could have purchased ready-mixed doll enamel from the local dolls' hospital, but she wanted to experiment. The result was perfect. Elsie was delighted.

"Nothing succeeds like success." Mother thought of Jennie, great grandmother's doll lying neglected in an attic trunk. A large part of its papiér

13. Jennie. An Old Papier Mache-Headed Doll Restored.

mâché head was missing, and the shoulders completely gone. "Now, I wonder what kind of shoulders?" she mused. "Ah, I know. I will look in the book 'Dolls—A Guide for Collectors;' that will give me a cue." It did. She found the type and the period of the doll, and the rest was fun. First she filled the head to within a quarter inch of the top with Scot toweling, then ran a stick from the center of the head through the body of the doll (see chapter on "The Story of Alice and Mabel"), and the head was in position to be worked on. After cutting a pattern of Scot toweling for the shoulder, she pasted it in position and proceeded with the job of reconstruction, using the same mixture she had used for Elsie's doll.

It was a difficult task to handle so large a mass of the plastic, but by skillful manipulation, smoothing over with the flat of a knife blade, afterwards trimming the edges neatly, she finally managed a creditable achievement.

The missing head part was much easier to restore. An orange stick helped in modeling the hair, and when it was painted to blend with the rest of the coiffure, only an experienced eye could detect the mend.

Many china dolls come to the collector in lamentable condition. Such was the case with Editha, a common china-head of the "gay nineties" period. But Editha was not gay. Both china hands had been broken off, most of one foot was missing, and the other completely gone. Further than this, Editha had no clothes, not even a little chemise, a truly neglected child of another era. But in this modern day she would be taken care of. A new set of arms and legs might have been purchased through the offices of Mrs. Emma C. Clear, well

14. Editha, A Restored China-Headed Doll.

known to collectors as the foremost mender of dolls in the United States. But the new owner of Editha felt she could not wait for that. Looking up the period of the doll, so as to get the correct style, she proceeded to carve (see chapter "On Carving and Modeling Dolls") a new set of legs and arms. The illustration shows Editha in her former dilapidated state, the kind of arm and leg carved, and an appropriate dress made of old materials found in the Washington, D. C., Thrift Shop. Underclothes similar to those illustrated in the chapter "The Story of Alice and Mabel" also were made. And Editha took her place among respectable dolls in a good collection.

Mary Ann (see illustration) arrived at the home of her collector mother minus a part of one foot. A modeling job would do for this, but first an armature for the foot was necessary. This was made by covering a small piece of wire tightly with Scot toweling and pasting the ends together. One end was thrust up through the shallow inside part of the leg, the other end bent into the position of a foot. Plastic, in this case, was made with dentists' plaster mixed with wallpaper paste. A lump of the mixture was pressed firmly over the paper-covered wire and modeled carefully. After drying and painting to match the perfect foot, the new owner of Mary Ann was quite pleased with herself—and with the doll. The latter was of an earlier period than Editha, for she boasted the flat-soled foot which proclaims the pre-Civil War period. The dress shown in the illustration is an original.

15. Mary Ann (China-Head) and Her Mended Foot.

The most serious trouble with Atrocia, a wax-over-papiér-mâché doll which came to another collector, was not only its dirty condition, but half the wax was gone, evidently gnawed off by mice, for little teeth marks showed all around the edges. No wonder the doll was named Atrocia. The first problem—to remove all the wax from the head—was simply solved by plunging the head into hot wax. Adding one orange and one red candle to a washpail full of cream colored (white would have done) candle ends purchased for a cent apiece at the Goodwill Industries, the pail was placed over a slow gas burner and brought to the steaming point. Then the head was immersed quickly and immediately brushed off with a soft cloth. Presto! A clean head! But the face was pale, much too pale in the places where the mice had done their work. Re-waxing could not be done for another month, for Atrocia had to be restored to her original beauty with the help of the artist's aid to loveliness—oil paint, in this instance, carefully blended into cheeks. This had to "set" thoroughly; otherwise the paint would appear blotchy under a freshly waxed surface. And so the wax in the pail cooled off while Atrocia underwent a beauty treatment, and then was put away for awhile. When the time came for her to be re-dipped, the wax was made not quite so hot as previously, and the dipping (crown first, of course) not quite so hurried. It often helps to re-dip after the head has cooled somewhat. After each dipping, the eyes must be carefully stripped of wax. This may be done with the little finger nail and a tiny pocket knife. Care must be taken that the edges are smooth; fuzzy eyes on a wax doll are not attractive. If the wig is placed on the head immediately, no glue will be necessary, as the hot wax does

16. Atrocia (Wax) Becomes Cecelia.

the trick, but if you have no wig and are planning to buy one later on, as was the case with Atrocia, it is well to scrape off the wax which would come underneath the wig, for wax will not take kindly to glue. Experiment with a stick before dipping the head to be waxed, so as to get the right temperature.

When Atrocia was completely finished and a suitable wig found, her name was changed to Cecelia, for she was far too lovely to be called anything implying ugliness. The title of this little story might be "Why Atrocia Changed Her Name."

Geraldine came to her present owner with all her sixteen parts completely unstrung, but lovely enough to be restored and cherished by even the most ex-

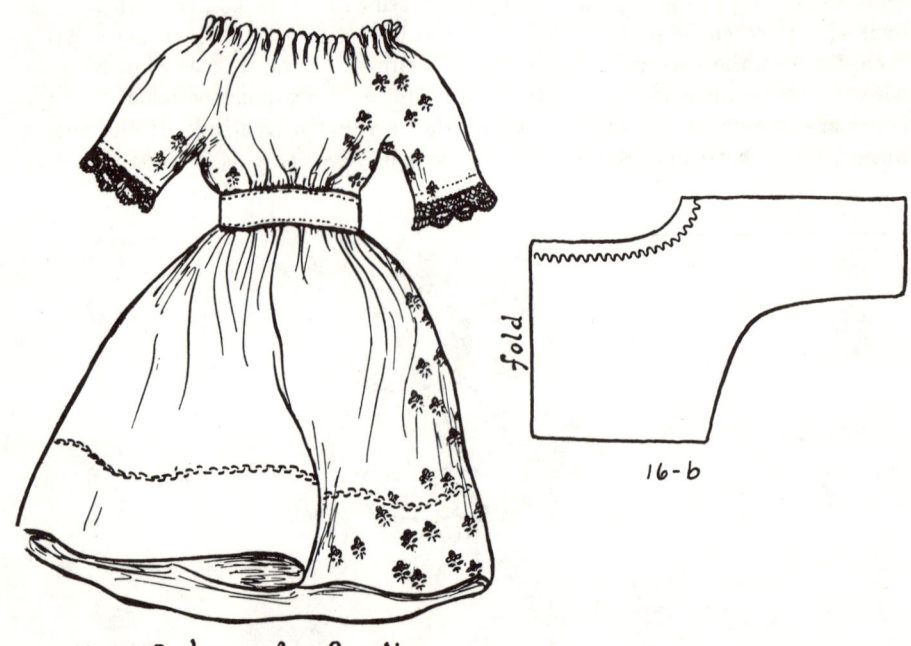

16-a A dress for Cecelia

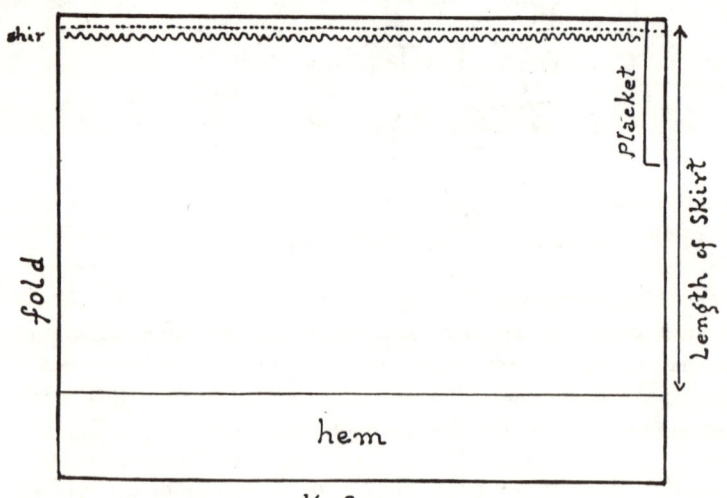

16-c: A Dress For Cecelia.

acting collector. There are vast differences in beauty and quality among these bisque-headed jointed dolls that were so popular in the late nineteenth and early twentieth centuries. Their popularity lasted a long time. Millions were made between the 1880's and the 1930's. In the later years there were few left in American department stores; modern composition had taken their place. Of all the so-called "antique" dolls, these are the easiest for collectors to find. The closed-mouth variety usually are the prettiest, and they are apt to be earlier. Most of those we find today are, of course, not the earliest of their type.

17 - Geraldine in a girl's
Apron dress of 1885

17. Geraldine, A Jointed Doll.

Geraldine is a particularly fine one. (Note the closed mouth and good proportions.) She was made by the Kestner Company in Germany, a firm almost as noted for fine dolls as the famous French Jumeau.

A study of the diagram 17-b will show exactly how the doll was put together. First a good strong elastic—the kind used for making loops in fur coats—was purchased at the Washington Button Shop. At that time, Jack's Fixit Shop, a dolls' hospital, did not have the right size for sixteen-inch Geraldine, for this was during a war when many things were scarce.

Notice that the elastic is looped double around the knee hook marked 1, brought up through the ball joint and the hollow upper leg and body, looped over the hook at the base of the neck (2), brought down again through the body and then through the opposite leg to the knee hook marked 3, where it is tied firmly to the hook. The elastic in the arms is managed in the same manner, except that it is not passed through the neck hook.

An important thing to remember when stringing dolls is that the elastic must be pulled as tightly as possible; otherwise after the tie is made the limbs will be hopelessly loose. Useful tools in restringing dolls are a pair of pliers for opening up hooks that are too tightly pressed together, and a button hook or hooked wire for drawing the elastic through the openings in the body and limbs.

Geraldine's dress (17) was taken from Pattern No. 9818 in "The Delineator" for 1885. In those days a winter apron, such as this, was used as a dress

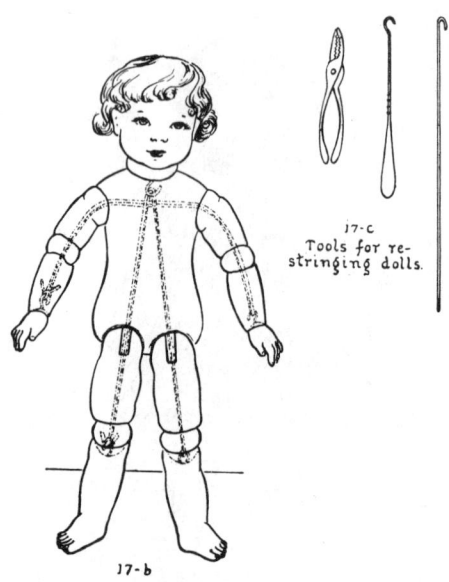

17-b: Geraldine Restrung.
17-c: Tools Used in Re-stringing Dolls.

17-a: Geraldine in Sixteen Parts.

in the summer time. Notice the pansy print, popular at this time. The shoes are typical. If the doll had represented an older child, she would have worn heels.

No. 18, Dorothy Dee, is a French doll (Jumeau child) of about the same period as Geraldine. She has her original costume. Note the short skirt. In the late nineteenth century European children wore shorter skirts than their American cousins. Dorothy's is a particularly attractive little outfit. The basque is

18. Dorothy Dee. A French Jointed Doll in Original Outfit.

of plum-colored silk brocade piped with yellow satin, once rather bright. The shirred front is of the same yellow satin. Lace trims the neck and sleeves. Dorothy has a wide pleated skirt of plum-colored satin. Her bonnet is the same shade, but of velvet, and is trimmed with pleated light blue satin ribbon over ruching around the face, topped with a jaunty ribbon bow. Slippers have metal buckles and buttons. Dainty underwear shows beneath the costume. Altogether, her ensemble represents a perfect example of the dressmaker's art in miniature. One would go a long way to find such careful workmanship in a child's doll of today.

Tommy (No. 19) a German doll of 1927, has modeled hair parted on the side in true boyish fashion. His original body, jointed like Geraldine's, was entirely missing when the present owner found him in an old-established dolls' hospital (now out of business) in New York City. Since no body of exactly the right size and style could be found, the deficiency was supplied in an amateur,

19. Tommy, A Bisque Swivel Head Which Needed a Body.

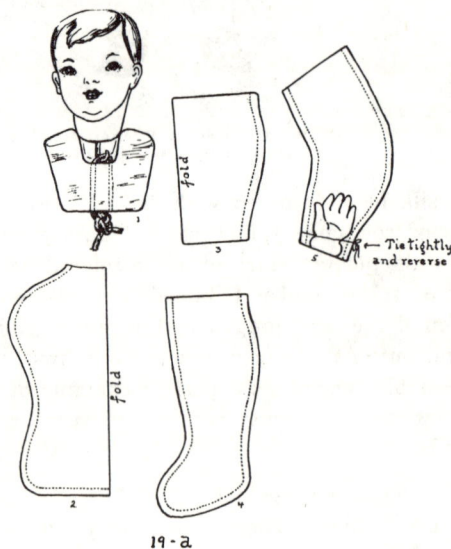

19-a: How Tommy Was Fitted Together.

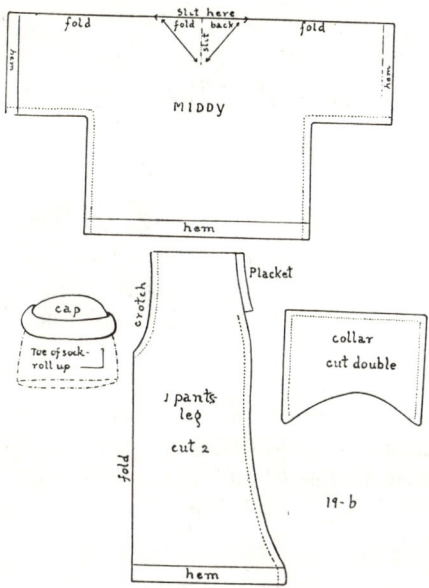

10-b: Clothes for Tommy.

yet effective way. Diagram No. 1 shows how the head was attached to a wooden base to be placed inside the chest of a cloth body. Through the groove, made just wide enough for the head to rest on the shoulders, two holes were drilled. A piece of elastic then was run through the hole at lower right, caught up over the neck hook, and run down through the hole at left, the two ends tied tightly at the base.

Diagram 2 shows half the front of the body. Cut two of these double on the fold.

Bisque hands were found in a dolls' hospital in Philadelphia; some of these may be found in your own neighborhood. Place the hand in position as shown in Diagram 5. Tie tightly at the groove in the wrist and reverse so that the hand will be in normal position and the seams inside.

Proceed with the leg parts (3 and 4) as described in Chapter II.

No. 19 shows Tommy finished and dressed. His middy-blouse is very simple to make. Cut (19-a) double on the fold, slit straight across center neckline, and down the middle of the front to the points of the arrows. Turn back and attach the collar straight around the neckline. Dotted lines show the parts to be stitched, straight lines represent the hem. The cap, Diagram 19-d, is the toe of a white sock, the lower part rolled up to form the brim. Diagram 19-b, represents one-half of Tommy's trousers. Proceed with this as in Chapter III.

Chapter V

The Story of Alice and Mabel
or
The Restoration of a Parian Bisque Doll

THE dolls, "Alice" and "Mabel," namesakes of their original owners, two sisters, were given the little girls in the year 1880, when the latter were above five and six years old respectively. Sketches of the children are based on photographs made in March, 1881.

"Alice" was the first of the dolls to join her present household. She belonged to the younger sister, Alice Goddard. And Alice is a story in herself. She still works in a New England hospital, where, she says, "I am nursing because they need me—I have retired from the profession." This frail little

20. Alice and Mabel, Twin Dolls.

woman, herself needing care, gives all she has to those worse off than herself "because they need me." And perhaps that is why she keeps young. The need of being needed is everything; when that is gone, everything is gone. And so, at an age when most of us sit back and say "Now I have done my duty, it is time to rest," Alice still carries on in the true tradition of her valiant New England ancestors who never failed to give their "last full measure of devotion" to a needful cause. We have reason to be proud of America and New England in particular.

In the summer of 1947, the writer was invited by Miss Goddard to the above mentioned hospital to see "a doll's head" and a box of tiny garments that belonged to twin dolls.

The nurse received her guest in a private office off the main hall and opened a carefully wrapped package. Apologizing for the missing shoulders of the doll, she took from the box one of the best examples of nineteenth century doll heads one would wish to see. And, one by one, placed on the desk before her, little underclothes yellowed by time, and carefully-made outer garments worn threadbare in places, but still fine examples of the patient needlecraft of other years. There were small quilts, too, and other accessories.

Miss Goddard told of her childhood with her older sister, and a stepmother who brought them up. They were motherless as tiny children. The new mother was good and kind, but with fixed ideas of duty toward her young charges. Mabel, who left this earth under heavenly escort in 1938, suffered from childhood with a serious physical handicap. But the perfectly healthy Alice, with tears streaming down her face, must stitch by hand one square of a quilt each day before she might go out and play. Mother, however, lessened the pain by the promise of a silver thimble if the little girl would do her sewing without weeping for a whole month. Alice, with remarkable fortitude for a six-year-old, won out and Mother, of course, kept her word.

One of the children's quilts is reproduced on page 41. The squares, probably made up, at least in part, from scraps of their own small dresses, give an idea of prints of the period and may be helpful in dating a garment.

The beautiful dolls played a large part in the lives of Alice and Mabel. They accompanied them on walks through the wood with their beloved father. "In trying to recall memories of my childhood," Miss Goddard says, "I find nearly everything revolved about my father, who seemed the center of my universe. After his death, when I was ten, there were few highlights, although my stepmother, with rare devotion to my sister and myself, kept the home together through many difficulties.

"One of my early recollections was of an evening when Mabel and I were playing about the living room—'sitting room' we called it then. Papa, who was somewhat gifted as a poet, was working on a poem dedicated to my eldest brother, who died when he was nine. Evidently feeling left out, I teased Papa to write something for Mabel and me. So he put aside his work and soon had on paper a jingle called 'A Song for Mabel and Alice.' Great was our delight and pride when it was included in a small book he later had printed for his friends called 'Buds, Briars and Berries.'

"When I was about seven my father, who disliked cities, bought a sixty-acre farm about three miles from Worcester, driving daily to his office. We lived there until his death, and high among my memories are the walks we (including the dolls) took with our father. He showed us witch hazel in blossom with the snow still on the ground, and pointed out where dogtooth violets, maiden-hair fern and rarer plants could be found. He was quick to detect the rustle of partridges in the brush, or prints of small animals in the snow, and would tell us to keep 'very still' until they came from their hiding places. On rare occasions he would set up his small telescope in the yard and point out the stars and tell us their names.

"On some of the 'big' days, such as birthdays, etc., when we had a special supper, our dolls had places of honor at the table. I remember one night Papa came in with our little maltese kitten we called Plush, curled up fast asleep in a wee basket, and put it in the middle of the table as a centerpiece, much to our delight and Mamma's dismay.

"On Sunday evenings in the summer, Papa would move the old-fashioned melodeon which graced our parlor, out under the big ash trees in the yard, and with Mamma at the keyboard, and my sister and I perched with our dolls on the arms of Papa's chair, we would sing lustily, if not musically, the old songs and hymns.

"With perhaps a forecast of my future work 'my dolly,' which is all I remember calling her, had to endure many illnesses. One day I informed the household she was very sick with 'new ammonia.' I explained that in spite of all I could do, she would get the ammonia bottle and smell of it until she came down with a dreadful cough.

"Mabel and I both were very shy and often shamed our Mother by refusing to look up or tell our names when among strangers. But Mabel, in spite of her handicap, developed a wonderful capacity for making and keeping friends. I still hear from one she met on her first day in school. They were always 'best friends.'"

A month went by; the writer returned to her home in the District of Columbia contented with the thought of "Alice" tucked carefully away in a suitcase. Then came a happy message. Miss Goddard had found her sister Mabel's doll, the twin of "Alice;" it was complete and dressed in an original costume similar to one of "Alice's."

No time was lost in mending the shoulder of the broken doll and making a body for her. The latter was patterned exactly after that of the other doll.

While both of them have their original clothes, it was decided that the dolls should have new "old-fashioned" dresses, for they were to be a Christmas present for Claire Fawcett, and their old garments, moth-eaten, would scarcely suit a festive occasion. Some especially beautiful English figured broadcloth had been saved for a number of years for that "super" doll a collector always feels sure of one day acquiring. The material was just enough (by patching) to make a "Gabrielle" or "Princess" gown for each doll. The original owners should have seen their restored darlings, one standing, one seated in a miniature chair, under the gayest of Christmas trees, the center of attraction among the numerous presents incident to the season. We hope Mabel's spirit was hovering near. Alice had a good idea of the scene from a photograph made especially for her.

Those who have a treasured casualty such as "Alice" will want to know how she was restored. Of course, one may shift the responsibility to a reliable mender of bisque, but there always is the possibility that something may go wrong at the mender's and that the coloring may be impaired. It was decided not to run this risk, especially since the doll could be dressed in such a way that it would hide completely a mend in the shoulders.

After a careful examination of "Mabel's" body, and measurements taken, Diagrams 20-a were cut. No. 1, one-half the front and upper leg, is cut double.

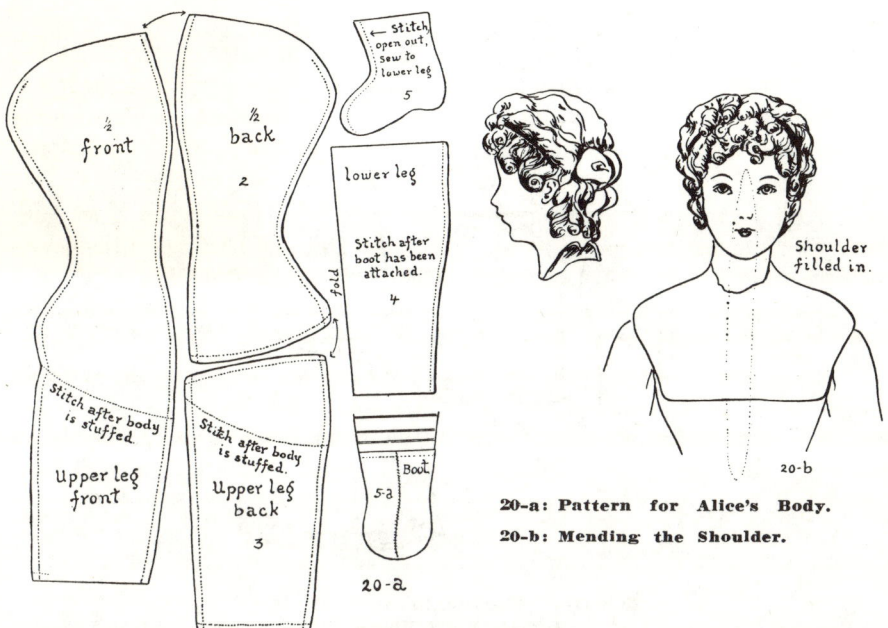

20-a: Pattern for Alice's Body.
20-b: Mending the Shoulder.

Nos. 2 and 3, one-half the back, is cut double and stitched together as indicated in the diagram. The front and back halves are then stitched together, first down the middle seams, then at the sides, and lastly at the rump. This leaves the top open to the rump, and the lower leg-uppers open at the bottom for stuffing. (Sawdust is the best of all stuffing for dolls of any head weight.) The body should receive the first stuffing. Now sew at the top so that the sawdust will not spill out when you turn the body upside down and stuff the upper legs. Sew up the bottom part of these upper leg parts.

Cut two of No. 4 (lower leg) double on the fold and press out so that the fold is in the center of the lower leg. Join to 5-b so that the foot will be in position, then stitch the back seam to complete lower leg and boot. The lines to represent a striped stocking are made with Higgins blue ink. Any color, of course, may be used.

20-b shows how the broken head of "Alice" was held in position on the body by means of a stick running from the head through the bust. The head was first stuffed with paper to hold the stick in place.

Dentists' plaster mixed with wallpaper paste to form a clay-like substance is used to model the shoulders. This is flattened out and smoothed with a flexible table knife, and neatly trimmed around the edges. The shoulders of a doll like this are deep and sloping.

20-c (1 to 3) represents underwear belonging to the twin. Cut No. 1 (the chemise) double on the fold and stitch as indicated. The fold may be on the

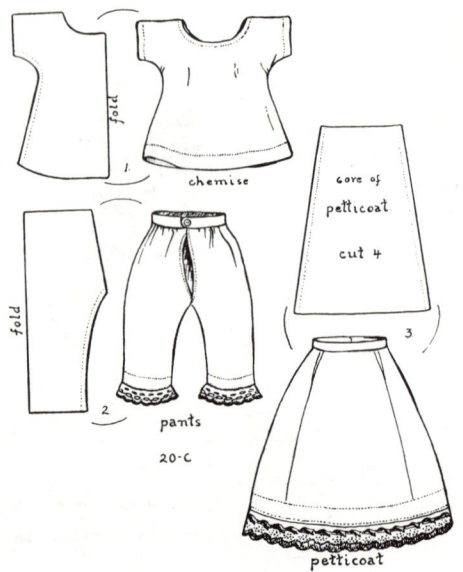

20-c (1-3): Chemise, Pants, Petticoat
for Alice and Mabel.

shoulders. In that case make a pattern showing the complete front. Cut wide enough at the top for the head to pass through, and low enough for your doll to wear the chemise under a low-necked dress.

Cut No. 2, the trousers, double on the fold for each pants-leg. Sew the front middle seam from the crotch to the waist, but leave the back open at this point, as shown in the sketch.

Notice the old-fashioned embroidery. 20-d and 20-e represent the embroidery on the "best petticoats" of "Alice" and "Mabel" respectively.

20-f, a princess dress for the twin, (a style that has survived to this day) was cut from the same pattern as that used for the Christmas dresses, No. 20. It was made from Pattern No. 20-g (1-3). Cut No. 1 double on the fold. Flattened out, it will represent the front panel, center. The back center panel is cut from the same pattern except that a wider margin is allowed on the fold, and the neck is cut higher. The wider margin is allowed to take care of a hem which must be made when the placket is cut from the middle of the neck to a point low enough below the waist so that the dress may be slipped on over the head.

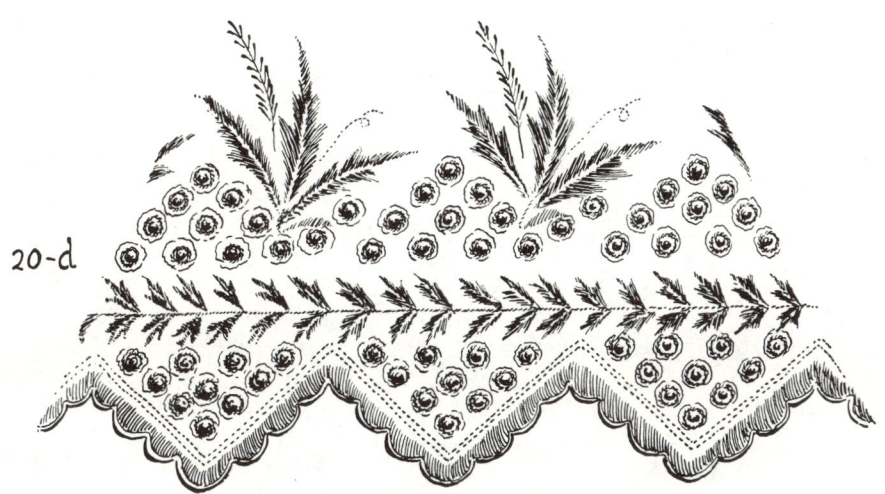

20-d: Embroidery on Alice's Best Petticoat.

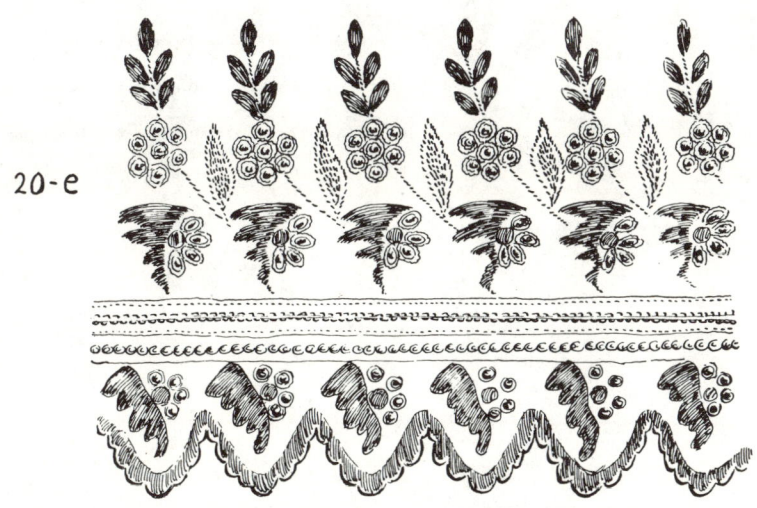

20-e: Embroidery on Mabel's Best Petticoat.

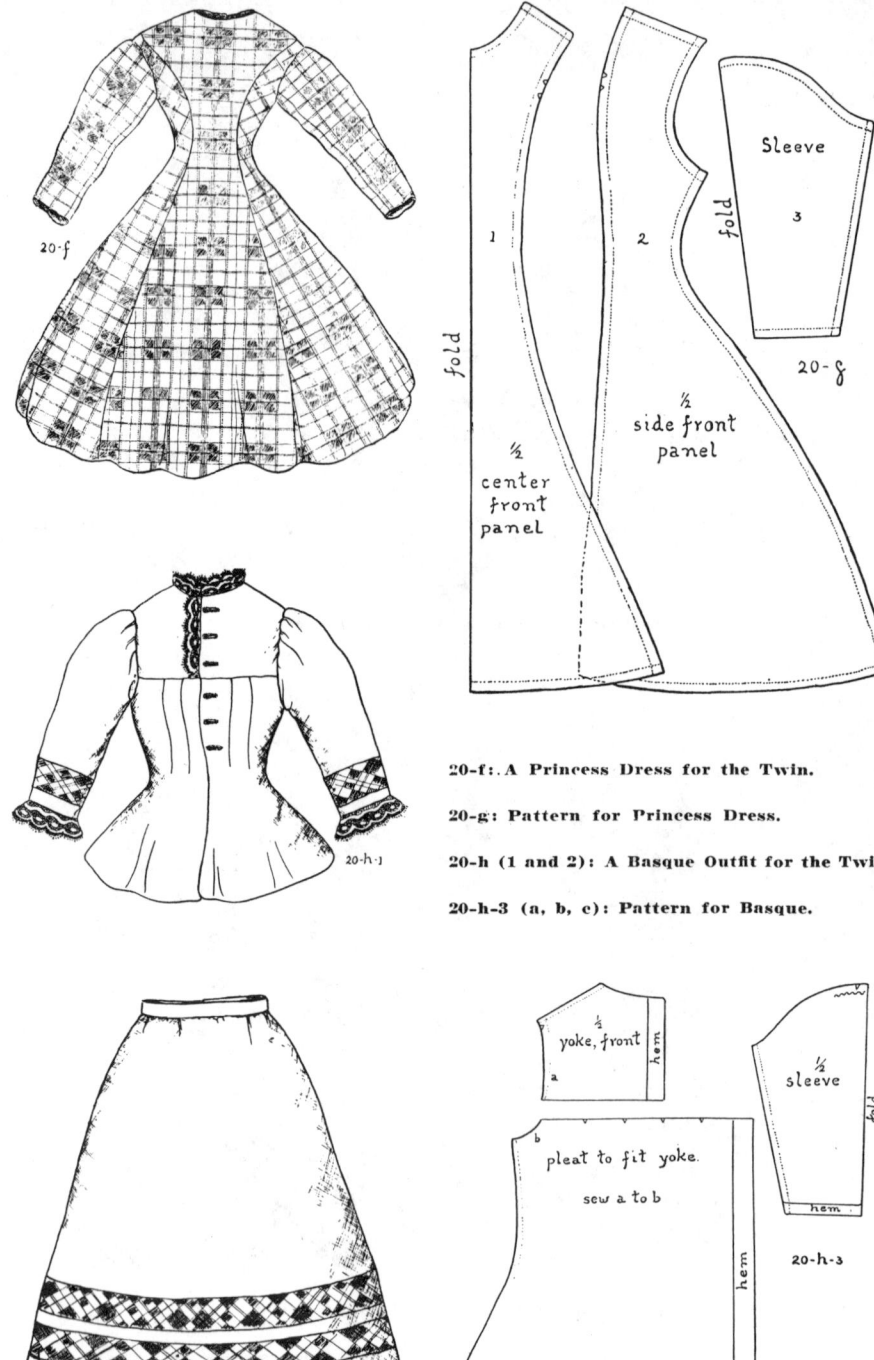

20-f: A Princess Dress for the Twin.

20-g: Pattern for Princess Dress.

20-h (1 and 2): A Basque Outfit for the Twin.

20-h-3 (a, b, c): Pattern for Basque.

Cut No. 2, the side front panel, double, one of each piece to be stitched to either side of the front panel. The same panel may be used for the back, the sleeve opening changed slightly as shown by the dot-and-dash line in the diagram. Treat the cutting of the sleeve (No. 3) in the same way. Cut double on the fold. The material is a fine plaid cotton.

20-h (1 and 2), a basque outfit for the twin was made of tan bombazine (a mixture of silk and cotton) trimmed with blue and tan plaid bandings of the same texture. The basque is further embellished with old-fashioned lace at neck, yoke and sleeves.

20-h-3 (a, b and c) is the pattern for the basque. Cut two of a (one-half the front yoke) which includes a hem at the opening. Use the same pattern for the back yoke, eliminating the extra strip allowed for the hem at center front,

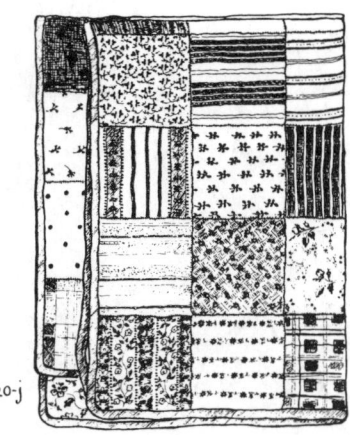

20-j: A Quilt for Alice.

and cutting the neckline a little higher. Fold at the inside line on the diagram and cut double. Treat pattern b in the same manner. Notches show where the pleats come. C represents one-half the sleeve. Cut double on the fold. Join notches at yoke and sleeve and shirr slightly at top of sleeve.

Pattern 20-i (1 and 2) represents another style for a basque outfit. This was made up in woolen material, hence the bulky look of the finished basque, which is copied from the original.

20-i-3 is the pattern for the basque. No. 1 is half the front and should be cut double. No. 2 is half the back, which should also be cut double and joined at center seam. 3 is the upper part of the sleeve, and 3-a the lower. Join at notches.

The skirt, 20-i-2, is plain gored (see No. 11) with peplum, 20-i-4, added. Shirr peplum at the point indicated by wavy line in diagram and join to waistline, first overlapping peplum at center front, as sketched.

20-j is a sketch of Alice's little quilt, size eleven by fifteen inches. Mabel's quilt is made in the same way, but many of the squares are of different prints.

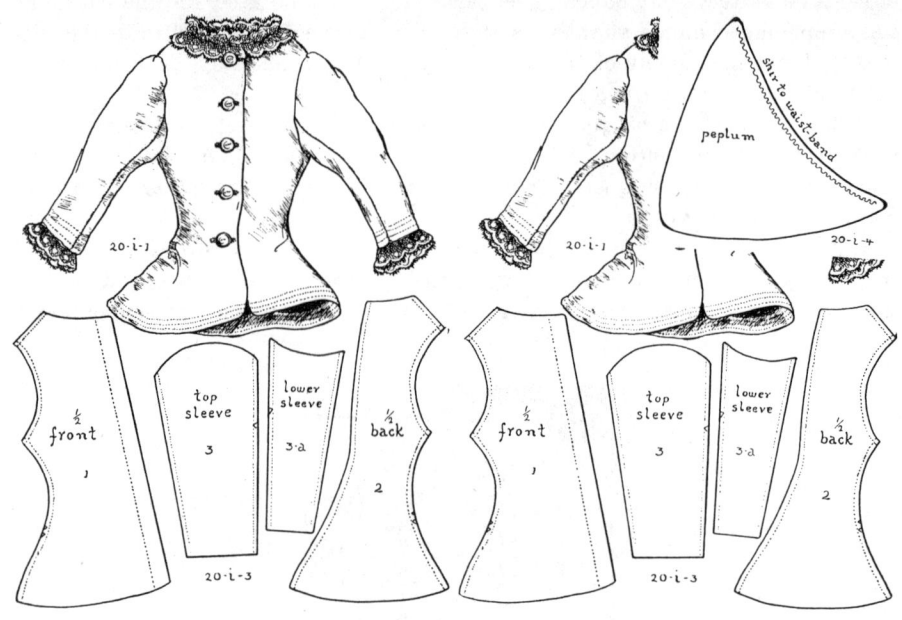

Costume for Mabel and Alice.

The patterns at upper left and right are identical except that the one on the right includes the skirt peplum, while the one at the left shows the full jacket.

What a story is bound up in each small quilt! If the squares could speak, they might tell of childish joy in a new dress—many new dresses for the children, some for the mother and step-mother. The work is beautifully done, the patches

Mabel and Alice in person, from old portraits.

sewn together by hand and stitched afterward, one to a plain, the other to a figured background, the whole piped with red cotton. Both are in splendid condition and probably will last another seventy years.

Chapter VI

The Story of Private Robert Edward Ball
or
The Restoration of a China Doll

ON a shelf among the most prized possessions of Claire Fawcett, is a little twelve-inch china doll dressed as a Union soldier. He has a knapsack on his back and a sword in his belt and stands guard over a cosmopolitan array of distinguished antique dolls, each with a story of its own and a place in the heart of the owner. But it is the story of Robert Edward which interests us most.

Dressed as a Union soldier, he was put up for sale at a Sanitary Fair in Zanesville, Ohio, to raise money for the cause of the Union. Proudly he stood at attention while prospective customers came and went. Most of them purchased the girl dolls, of which there was quite a showing. No one wanted Robert until the advent of General William H. Ball. "Aha!" said the General, "A soldier and gentleman! Just the thing for my two-year-old son, Robert Edward, I will take him; wrap him up."

And so the doll, now Robert Edward, arrived at the home of the Ball family, amid squeals of delight from the children, a boy and a girl, and there he remained for twenty-six years, serving first one member of the family, then another. In Civil War days his only name was "Soldier Boy." He was the favorite doll of the youngsters, caressed, admonished, tucked nightly into bed. However he survived the onslaughts of that two-year-old is a wonder. But we shall allow "Soldier Boy" to tell his story in his own way:

"When the Ball children went to Winchester, just before the battle of Antietam, I remember Robert Edward's sister being placed upon a big white horse with me in her arms. The soldiers came flocking round to speak to 'Sister,' and she held me up for them to see.

"Visiting with Grandmother Ball was Colonel Granger's wife, at that time only eighteen years old, and a famous beauty. Word came sooner than expected that the battle of Antietam Creek was to be fought. Suddenly on the boards at our feet Mother Ball noticed dark spots. Puzzled, she look at Mrs. Granger, who stood with bowed head. The dark spots were tears from the eyes of the young wife.

"I got to know the soldiers very well, for when we visited our father, General Ball, I was taken along. Father Ball was a friend of General Sheridan, and in later years never tired of telling stories of the great General, and of how the soldiers loved him. Once, when they were encamped, word came that General Sheridan was coming. Instantly every soldier left his bacon frizzling in the pan and rushed to meet his leader.

The Story of Private Robert Edward Ball

"During these Civil War days, I was taken to Miss Pike's day school for little boys and girls, and I remember the teacher suffered from food shortage. At that time flour was $50 a half barrel, and coffee a great luxury. The teacher made what she called coffee with a kind of toasted sawdust.

"The war passed, the children grew up. I was put away for awhile to reminisce on the stirring events of my life. Then came a grandchild, Mildred, and in 1888 I was passed on to her. By that time, my clothes were literally 'played out.' Shame of shames! I was dressed in girls' clothes and my perfectly good name changed to Alice. Imagine the feelings, if you can, of a fine, full-bodied boy doll, and a soldier at that, dressed as a girl and called Alice.

"During the Spanish-American War I wore the costume of a nurse, but was aching to once more don the uniform of a soldier. One comfort remained. Mildred loved me all through her childhood, and even into adult life, and together we have traveled from one end of this Union to another, at first in a little round-topped trunk with my various belongings, then in a pretty bag with pink and black wool trimmings.

"When Mildred grew up she married, and in 1919 I was passed on to her son, William Dugan. World War I was over, but its influence remained, and I was clothed in the olive drab and knitted sweater of a more modern American soldier. My original personality re-established, I should have been happy, but Master Dugan cared not for dolls, even soldier dolls. He much preferred a stuffed elephant—ugly thing—which he called 'Plushie.' At the time, my feelings were hurt, but now I am content, for otherwise I might not have survived—who knows? At any rate, Mildred still cared for me, even though my poor body had become a wreck in the battle of life (literally loved to pieces) and my saw-

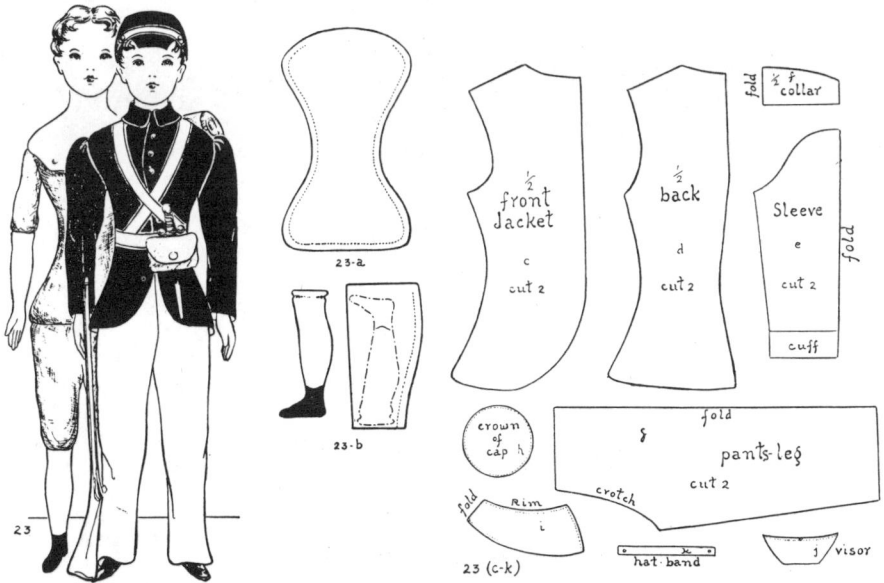

23. Private Robert Edward Ball. 23-a: Body Pattern. 23-b: Leg. 23-(e-k): Pattern for "Soldier Boy" Outfit.

dust 'blood' was strewn to the four winds. And now, fearful of what might happen if I still accompanied her in her wanderings, she has given me into the custody of a real doll lover, Claire Fawcett, who, recognizing my true character, has re-dressed me in the costume of the Union Soldier after persuading her mother to give me a reconstruction job. It was Claire who gave me my present name—Private Robert Edward Ball, after my original owner. Recently, however, she has been thinking of elevating my rank. 'For' she says 'a soldier who has survived four major wars without once losing his head should certainly be at least a general.'"

No. 23 shows "Soldier Boy" in his uniform, and the type of body made for him. Pattern 23-a is cut double, stitched as indicated, reversed and stuffed. He has a china arm, but the lower legs are carved after the original style and fastened to a cloth upper as previously described. (See 23-b)

Patterns 23, c-k, represent Robert Edward's jacket, trousers and cap. Cut two of c (half the front) and cut d (half the back) double on the fold. Cut two of e (the sleeve) and f (half the collar) double on the fold. A space is left at the bottom of the sleeve to form the cuff. G is "Soldier Boy's" pants-leg. Proceed with this as previously described in making trousers. H is the small crown of the cap. I, the side part which covers the head, should be cut double on the fold and stitched at the back before attaching (the smaller rim is uppermost) to the crown. Attach the visor (j) and fasten on the front band (k) with tiny round brass paper fasteners to represent buttons. The coat was made with dark blue thin cotton flannel, the trousers of the same material but a lighter shade. The cap is made of dark blue felt, and the visor is thin black leather. Blanket roll is grey wool; straps and pouch, tan kid from a glove. Round paper fasteners, such as were used for the cap, form buttons for the coat.

Chapter VII

Suggestions for Nineteenth Century Doll Costumes

A PERFECTLY preserved antique doll in a quaint or lovely original gown is, of course, the aim of the collector, but when this is not possible, one of old material as near to the period of the doll in line and cut as possible is appropriate. It is difficult to find just the right cloth, but persistence will reap rewards. An old attic trunk, the Thrift Shop, the Goodwill Industries or the Morgan Memorial, as it is called in the Boston area, are all sources of supply. Old and faded brocades reflecting past elegance are still procurable; so also the quaint calicos of a bygone generation.

A study of such books as Elizabeth McClellan's "History of American Costume," "English Costume From the Fourteenth Through the Nineteenth Century" by Iris Brooke and James Laver, old copies of Godey's "Lady's Book," "Peterson's Magazine," "Harpers," etc., furnish authentic information, and it is hoped that this chapter will be of some help to those in search of ideas. Since most of the old dolls still extant are of the period between 1850 and 1900, emphasis will be given the costume of these years.

Hair styles, as well as the general contour of the face and neck, furnish clues to suitable costuming. Don't dress your antique "child" as a "lady" unless it represents a period when children were dressed like adults—before 1815.

Dolls of the First Empire Period are very rare. When we find a doll of about 1800, it is apt to have the plain hairdo of the period. Short hair was fashionable. The ultra stylish often wore wigs of short curls.

With regard to early nineteenth century dress, Mrs. Merrifield, in "The Art-Journal" (an English publication) of 1853 refers back to the Empire period in this wise: "The first fashion we remember was that of scanty clothing, when slender figures were so much admired, that many to whom nature had denied this qualification, left off the under garments necessary for warmth, and fell victims to the colds and consumptions induced by their adoption of this senseless practice. To these succeeded waists so short, that the girdles were placed almost under the arms, and as the dresses were worn at that time indecently low in the neck, the body of the dress was almost a myth.

"About the same time the sleeves were so short, and the skirts so curtailed in length that there was reason to fear that the whole of the drapery might also become a myth; a partial re-action then took place, and the skirts were lengthened without increasing the width of the dresses, the consequence of which was felt in the country if not in the towns. Then woe to those who had to cross a ditch or a stile! one of two things was inevitable, either the unfortunate lady was thrown to the ground—and in this case it was no easy matter to rise again—or her dress was split up. The result depended entirely upon the strength of the materials of which the dress was composed. The next variation, the gigot sleeves,* namely, were a positive deformity, inasmuch as they gave an unnatural width to the shoulders, a defect which was further increased by the large collars which fell over them, thus violating one of the first principles of beauty in the female form, which demands that this part of the body should be narrow—breadth of shoulder being one of the distinguishing characteristics of the stronger sex. We remember to have seen an engraving from a portrait by Lawrence of the late Lady Blessington, in which the breadth of the shoulders appeared to be at least three quarters of a yard. When a person of low stature, wearing sleeves of this description, was covered with one of the long cloaks which were made wide at the shoulders to admit the sleeves, and to which was appended a deep and very full cape, the effect was ridiculous, and the outline of the whole mass resembled that of a hay-cock with a head on the top. One absurdity generally leads to another; to balance the wide shoulders, the bonnets and caps were made of enormous dimensions, and were decorated with a profusion of ribbons and flowers. So absurd was the whole combination that when we meet with a portrait of this period we can only look on it in the light of a caricature, and wonder that such should ever have been so universal as to be adopted at last by all who wished to avoid singularity. The transition from the broad shoulders and gigot sleeves to the tight sleeves and graceful black scarf was quite refreshing to a tasteful eye. These were a few of the freaks of fashion during the last half century. Had they been quite harmless, we might have considered them as merely ridiculous, but some of them were positively indecent, and others detrimental to health. We grieve especially for the former charge; it is an anomaly for which, considering the modest habits and education of our country-women, we find it difficult to account.''

There are extant, as we have mentioned before, dolls representing the later ''indecent'' period (1820's and 1830's) referred to by Mrs. Merrifield, notably those with papiér mâché heads, tiny waists, kid bodies and long slender wooden

24. **Gigot Sleeves of the 1830's From an Old Sketch.**

25. **1: Evening Dress. 2: Walking Dress.**

* See No. 24.

arms and legs. Costumes quaint and not too extreme taken from Godey's "Lady's Book" of 1828 are shown in sketch No. 25.

The drawing of Anne S. Stevens (No. 26) indicates that women of good taste could adapt the styles of 1835 in a most attractive manner.

Ridiculous hairdo (No. 27) shown on some of the early dolls reached their climax in the early eighteen thirties along with the enormous skirt and sleeve. The evening dress sleeve was so large that it had to be extended by means of wicker frames or small feather cushions.

Toward the close of the thirties, gowns for women were more picturesque, the ugly balloon sleeve gave way to the more graceful one wide below the elbow. There was a modified form of hoop, much more attractive than the exaggerated hooped skirt which was to appear later on. The fichu was replaced by collars of various shapes and sizes worn low and turned back. They were mostly of velvet

26. Costume of 1835. Anne S. Stevens, Editor of "The Portland Magazine," 1835.

27. Ridiculous Hairdos of the Early 1830's.

and watered silk, sometimes embroidered. Black silk mitts and embroidered colored handkerchiefs were stylish.

The poke bonnet, which made its appearance before the close of the eighteenth century, was almost universal by 1840. It became smaller, was pulled down at the sides closer to the face, and the crown lowered. In the middle forties, flowers were used on bonnets to such an extent that, according to "The Boston Transcript" of the period, looking down on a Sunday congregation was like gazing at a bed of roses and lilies. The changing shape of bonnet crown and brim during the century makes an interesting study. (See No. 28, "The Evolution of the Bonnet.")

The eighteen forties might be called the "petticoat era." Full skirts often harbored as many as six.

In men's clothes, black became the fashion. The flaring frock coat, tall hat and tight trousers made a quaint picture.

Brussels and Honitan lace was used extensively by ladies. It was of this lovely material that Queen Victoria's wedding gown was made (1840). Figure No. 29 shows a costume of 1840. The head is from a contemporary portrait of Queen Victoria.

Crinoline, and the sleeveless jacket called canagous was in vogue, the latter open in front and finished with a small collar trimmed with lace or embroidery. Redingotes (close fitting dresses) too, were popular. Sleeves were either tight or full, and the bodice pointed in front, round at the back. The low-necked evening gown with bertha of lace or of the same material as the dress, "Pompadour" sleeves, and a much be-flounced skirt, was considered elegant. Some of the sleeves for street dresses were finished with a jockey (epaulet) cap.

28. The Evolution of the Bonnet.   29. Costume of 1840.

This was a period of elaborate headgear made of India muslin or organdie, lace-trimmed. The back hair was braided or coiled low on the neck, while the front showed "broad braids, smooth bands, or long ringlets." Hair was parted in the middle, sometimes brought down severely on either side of the head, covering the ears, and coiled at the back. The "Polish braid" of nine strands carried across the head making a sort of coronet was so popular that it was reflected in the dolls. There are extant some interesting wax dolls with this hair arrangement. Evening hairdress was elaborate, with trimmings of flowers, jewels, ribbons, combs, etc. Coral ornaments, and a single gold "serpent" bracelet with ruby eyes adorned the right arm of a typical fashionable lady.

In the late eighteen forties and the eighteen fifties bonnets and parasols were small—see sketch No. 30-b. This "Walking Costume" is described in "Harper's" in 1850 as "an elegant promenade costume. The dress is a rich changeable brocade without flounces, trimmed in front with pinked ribbon, made in double knots. The body is high and the sleeves quarter length. Manteau of green satin or velvet, trimmed with black lace and rich silk guimpe. Bonnet of pink crape trimmed with satin; the form open; the bavolet, or curtain, very deep."

A high-necked house gown, described in "Harper's" also in 1850 as a "Home Dress," was finished with a tiny flat collar of lace or embroidery. Sleeves were long. The bodice opened in front over a white chemisette. An undersleeve to match the chemisete was a style which lasted twenty years. "Har-

30. "Home Dress" and "Walking Costume" of 1850.

31. Costume of 1845.

per's" still 1850 describes such a dress as "the gown en gros d'Ecosse with facing and trimmings cut out; pagode sleeves, with a white muslin puffing ornamented with a very large bouillonne." The dress referred to is Sketch No. 30, the head for which was taken from a contemporary portrait of Anna Cora Mowatt Ritchie, French author and actress.

"Harper's" goes on to tell of the "Pardessus and Mantelets, of the Pompadour style," which were then "in great request. Those intended for young women are principally composed of white, pink, English green, pearl-gray, and ecru silk. They are covered with embroideries formed by silk cord, representing Gothic patterns, Pompadours, and arabesques."

"Fashionable Colors. It is almost impossible to state which colors most prevail, . . . most in demand are maroon, sea-green, blue, pensee, etc."

Fashions did not change too often in earlier days. A costume of 1845, Figure 31, (from a contemporary portrait of Anne Charlotte Lynch, poet) might have been worn ten years later.

An ultra stylish doll of 1848 wore a long chain of beads or a cameo broach. If she were dressed for the street, the miniature "lady" might wear a new wrap like the mother of her small owner. The wrap, called a "Cornelia," could be gathered up on the arm like a shawl, for it had no shoulder seam. The long-waisted Josephine mantle with one cape, also had no shoulder seam. It, too, was popular.

Leghorn hats and chip bonnets were quite the thing. "Slippers," said a writer of the day "threaten to supersede gaiters for the street. The toes are rounded, and the instep ornamented with a small bow, quite as our grandmothers recollect them."

The "Quarterly Review" had this to say of dress in the forties:

"The present dress has some features worth dwelling on more minutely. The gown is a good thing, both in its morning and evening form, and contains all necessary elements for showing off a fine figure and a graceful movement. There is something especially beautiful, too, in the expanse of chest and shoulder, as seen in a tight plain-coloured high dress, merino or silk, like a fair sloping sunny bank, with the long taper arms and the slender waist so tempting and convenient between them, that it is a wonder they are not perpetually embracing it themselves. And then the long full folds of the skirt which lie all close together above, like the flutings of an Ionic column, as if loth to quit that sweet waist, but expand gradually below as if fearing to fetter those fairy feet. And the gentle swinging of the robe from side to side, like a vessel in calmest motion, and the silver whisper of trailing silk. Flounces are a nice question. We like them when they wave and flow as in a very light material, muslin or gauze or barege, when a lady looks like a receding angel, or a dissolving view; but we do not like them in a rich material where they flop, or in a stiff one, where they bristle; and where they break the lines of the petticoat, and throw light and shade where you don't expect them. In short we like the gown that can do without flounces, as Josephine liked a face that could do without whiskers; but in either case it must be a good one. The plain black scarf is come of too graceful a parentage—namely, the Spanish and Flemish mantilla—not to constitute one of the best features of the present costume. It serves to join the two parts of the figure together, enclosing the back and shoulders in a firm defined outline of their own, and flowing down gracefully in front, or on each side, to mix with that of the skirt. That man must be a monster who would be impertinent to a woman, but especially to a woman in a black scarf. It carries an air of self-respect with it which is in itself a protection. A woman thus attired glides on her way like a small close-reefed vessel, tight and trim, seeking no encounter but prepared for one. Much, however, depends on the wearer; indeed no article of dress is such a revealer of the wearer's character. Some women will drag it tight up their shoulders, and stick out their elbows (which ought not to be known to exist) in defiance at you, beneath. Others let it hang loose and listless like an idle sail, losing all the beauty of the outline, both moral and physical." Can any reader in 1949 imagine a modern writer having recourse to such ridiculous comparisons? The article continues: "Such ladies have usually no opinions at all, but none the less a very obstinate will of their own. Some few of what are nowadays called mantillas, which are the Cardinals and Capuchins of a century ago, are pleasing and blameless. A black velvet one turned up with a broad dull black lace, the bright metal chased with dead,* is very good. But whatever piece of dress conceals a woman's figure is bound in justice to do so in a picturesque way. That a shawl can never do with its stiff uniformity of pattern, each shoulder alike, and its

32. Gingham Dress of 1850.   33. Evening Dress of 1850.

stiff three-cornered shape behind with a scroll pattern standing straight up in the centre of the back. If a lady sports a shawl at all, and only very falling shoulders should venture, we should recommend it to be always either falling off or putting on, which produces pretty action, or she should wear it up one shoulder and down the other, or in some way drawn irregularly, so as to break the uniformity."

Figure 32 pictures a gingham dress of 1850. Usually the bodice at this time was pointed as in Figure 33. Figure 34 shows a hat and gown worn by Empress Eugenie in the same year. The sketches are of plain skirts, but flounces, too, were very popular, as many as five to a skirt, although for general wear, three was considered enough, the upper flounce gathered in with the skirt at the waist.

*Dull Metal.

Comments on low-cut evening dresses by Mrs. Merrifield back in 1853 make us smile, considering styles of today, especially in bathing suits. Mrs. Merrifield says: "It is singular that the practice of wearing dresses cut low around the bust should be limited to what is called 'full-dress,' and to the higher and, except in this instance, the more refined classes. Is it to display a beautiful neck and shoulders? No, for in this case it would be confined to those who had beautiful necks and shoulders to display. Is it to obtain the admiration of the other sex? That cannot be; for we believe that men look upon this exposure with unmitigated distaste, and that they are inclined to doubt the modesty of those young ladies who make so profuse a display of their charms. But if objectionable in the young, whose youth and beauty might possibly be deemed

34. Costume of 1850.

some extenuation, it is disgusting in those whose youth is past, whether their forms are developed with a ripe luxuriance which makes the female figures of Rubens appear in comparison slender and refined, or whether the yellow skin stretched over the wiry sinews of the neck remind one of the old women whom some of the Italian masters were accustomed to introduce into their pieces to enhance by contrast the beauty of the principal figures. Every period of life has a style of dress peculiarly appropriate to it, and we maintain that the uncovered bosom so conspicuous in the dissolute reign of Charles II, and from which, indeed, the reign of Charles I was not, as we learn from the Vandyck portraits, exempt, should be limited, even in its widest extension, to feminine youth or rather childhood.

"If the dress be cut low, the bust should be covered after the modest and becoming fashion of the Italian women, whose highly picturesque costume painters are so fond of representing."

A little farther on in the same publication, Mrs. Merrifield goes on to explain the failure of the Bloomer costume which had its origin in America. Mrs.

Bloomer was the editor of a temperance journal, and had ideas as to what the sensible woman should wear. The costume was worn in this country for a short time, but London laughed at the idea, the reason for which Mrs. Merrifield makes clear:

"We venture now to devote a few words to the Bloomer costume, although we are aware that this is treading on tender ground, especially as the costume involves a sudden and complete change in the dress. Independently of its merits or demerits, there were several reasons why it did not succeed in this country. In the first place, as we have before observed, it originated in America, and was attempted to be introduced through the middle ranks. In the second place, the change which it endeavored to effect was too sudden. Had the alteration commenced with the higher classes, and the change been effected gradually, its success might possibly have been different. Thirdly, the large hat so well adapted to the burning sun of America, was unnecessary and remarkable when forming part of the costume of adult ladies in this country, although we have seen that hats quite as large were worn during the time of Gainsborough. Another reason for the ill-success of the Bloomer costume is to be found in the glaring and frequently ill-assorted colours of the prints of it which were everywhere exposed in the shop-windows. By many sober-minded persons, the large hat and glaring colours were looked upon as integral parts of the costume. The numerous caricatures also, and the injudicious attempts to make it popular by getting up 'Bloomer balls,' contributed to render the costume ridiculous and unpopular.

"Setting aside the hat, the distinguishing characteristics of the costume are the short dress, and a polka jacket fitting the body at the throat and shoulders, and confined at the waist by a silken sash, and the trousers fastened by a band around the ancle,* and finished off with a frill. On the score of modesty there can be no objection to the dress, since the whole of the body is covered. On the ground of convenience it recommends itself to those who, having the superintendance of a family, are obliged frequently to go up and down stairs, on which occasions it is always necessary to raise the dress before or behind according to circumstances. The objection to the trousers is not to this article of dress being worn, since that is a general practice, but to their being seen. Yet we suspect few ladies would object on this account to appear at a fancy ball in the Turkish costume.

"The disadvantages of the dress are its novelty—for we seldom like a fashion to which we are entirely unaccustomed—and the exposure which it involves of the foot, the shape of which, in this country, is so frequently distorted by wearing tight shoes of a different shape from the foot. The short dress is objectionable in another point of view, because as short petticoats diminish the apparent height of a person, none but those who possess tall and elegant figures will look well in this costume; and appearance is generally suffered to prevail

---

* Old spelling.

over utility and convenience. If to the Bloomer costume had been added the long under-dress of the Greek women, or had the trousers been as full as those worn by the Turkish and East Indian women, the general effect of the dress would have been much more elegant, although perhaps less useful. Setting aside all considerations of fashion, as we always do in looking at the fashions which are gone by, it was impossible for any person to deny that the Bloomer costume was by far the most elegant, the most modest, and the most convenient.''

Salient features of spring fashions for 1850 can be gathered from the initial number of "Harper's New Monthly Magazine" for that year. The following is unsigned:

"There is a decided tendency in fashion this season to depart from simplicity in dress, and to adopt the extreme ornamental elegance of the middle ages. Bonnets, dresses, and mantles are trimmed all over with puffings of net, lace,

35. "Fashions for Early Summer." Sketched from "Harper's New Monthly Magazine," 1850.

and flowers. A great change has taken place in the width of skirts, which, from being very large, are now worn almost narrow. Ball dresses à tablier, apron trimming, as seen in the erect figure on the left,* are much in vogue, covered with puffings of net. Flounces of lace, forming the trimming of the bottom of the dress, have all a puffing of net at the top of them; the whole being fastened to the apron with a rosette of ribbon. A precious gem is sometimes worn in the centre of the rosette, either diamond, emerald, or ruby, according to the color of the dress. Wreaths are worn very full, composed of flowers and fruits of

---

* (Sketch 35, No. 1)

every kind; they are placed on the forehead, and the branches at the end of them are long, and fall on the neck. Bouquets, in shape of bunches, are put high up on the body of the dress. Such is the mania in Paris and London for mixing fruits of every kind, that some even wear small apples, an ornament far less graceful than bunches of currants, grapes, and tendrils of the vine. The taste for massive ornaments is so decided, that roses and poppies of enormous dimensions are preferred. For young persons, wreaths of delicate flowers, lightly fastened, and falling upon the shoulders, are always the prettiest.[1] Silks of light texture, in the styles which the French manufacturers designate chiné, will be generally employed for walking dresses until the extreme heat of summer arrives, when they will be superseded by French bareges, having flounces woven with borders, consisting of either satin stripes or flowers. Many of the patterns are in imitation of guipure lace. The most admired of the French light silks are those wrought upon a white ground, the colors including almost every hue. In some the ground is completely covered by rich arabesque patterns. These chinés, on account of the oriental designs, have obtained the name of Persian silks. Worsted lace is the height of fashion for mantles, which are trimmed with quillings of this article, plaited in the old style. The dresses are made with several flounces, narrower than last year, and more numerous. Nearly all the sleeves of visiting dresses are Chinese, or 'pagoda' fashion. The bodies are open in front, and laced down to the waist. Low dresses are made falling on the shoulders, and straight across the chest; others are quite square, and others are made in the shape of a heart before and behind. Opera polkas are worn short, with wide sleeves, trimmed with large bands of ermine.

"Broad-brimmed straw hats are used for the promenade; open-work straw bonnets, of different colors, are adopted for the earlier summer wear, trimmed with branches of lilac, or something as appropriate. White drawn silk bonnets, covered with foldings of net, are much worn. Also, drawn lace and crape bonnets, and black and white lace ones, are worn. Branches of fruit are much worn upon these last-mentioned bonnets. The tulip bonnet [2] is composed of white silk, covered with white spotted tulle; the edges of the front foliated, so as to give it a graceful and airy appearance. Many of the straw bonnets are of dark-colored ground, ornamented with fine open straw work. Crinoline hats, of open pattern, trimmed generally with a flower or feathers, are worn to the opera. They are exceedingly graceful in appearance, and make a fine accompaniment to a fancy dress.

"Elegant black lace jackets, with loosely-hanging sleeves, are worn, and form a beautiful portion of the dress of a well-developed figure. There is a style of walking dress, worn by those who have less love for ornaments. The robe is of a beautiful light apple-green silk, figured with white. The skirt is unflounced, but ornamented up the front with a row of green and white fancy silk buttons. Bonnet of pink crape, drawn in very full bouillonnées; strings of

---

[1] (No. 35—2)

[2] (Figure 35—3)

pink satin ribbon, and on one side a drooping boquet of small pink flowers. Corresponding boquets in the inside trimming. Shawl of pink China crape, richly embroidered with white silk.''

By 1853, women were copying the fashions of Empress Eugenie, whose magnificent costumes were the envy of all Europe. It is said that separate rooms were devoted to hats, bonnets, boots and shoes, sunshades, etc., and that each morning a life-sized doll made to the measurements of the Empress was carefully dressed, inspected by her, and changed to suit her taste.

Then came the return of the hoop-skirt, some made of graduated steel wires, covered, and held together by straps of tape, some simply lined with horsehair at the edges, the flounces with stiff muslin. Others used petticoats with casings into which canes were run. All this extra work ran up the prices, which meant fewer dresses for the majority.

A hundred dollars was quite a common price for a silk dress, and a bridal dress often sold for as high as $1,200; a fine bonnet for $200. The latter might have a cross-bar pattern in two shades of brown and with variegated pink roses en chiné. Deep collars came in and bonnets were worn back from the face. The cashmire shawl was even more in use than formerly.

From ''A Belle of the Fifties: Memoirs of Mrs. Clay, 1855-56,'' comes this information:

''In 1858-59 the hair was arranged on the top of the head in heavy braids, wound like a coronet, over the head and the coiffure was varied now and then with a tiara of velvet and pearls, or jet, or coral. Ruffled dresses gave place to panelled skirts in which two materials, a plain and embossed or brocaded fabric, were combined, and basques with postillion backs became the order of the day. The low-coiled hair, with brow free from frizzes and bangs, was the style adopted by such prominent beauties as Mrs. Pugh and Mrs. Pendleton, who in Lord Napier's opinion had the most classic head he had seen in America. Low necks and lace berthas, made fashionable because of their adoption by Miss Lane,* were worn almost universally, either with open sleeves revealing inner ones of filling lace, or sleeves of the shortest possible form allowing the rounded length of a pretty arm to be seen in all its perfection. Evening gloves were of half length only, or as often reaching half way to the elbow. They were of kid or silk with backs embroidered in delicate silks with now and then a jewel sparkling among the colours. Our gloves and our fans and handkerchiefs and bonnets and the larger part of our dress accessories, as well as such beautiful gown patterns as were purchased ready to be made up by a New York or Washington dressmaker, were all imported directly from foreign houses and the services of our travelling and consular friends were in constant requisition for the selection of fine lace shawls, flounces, undersleeves and other fashionable garnitures. Scarcely a steamer but brought to the Capital dainty boxes of Parisian flowers, bonnets and other foreign novelties despatched by such interested deputies.''

---

* Niece of President Buchanan

The hooped skirt began in rather picturesque fashion, but in the early sixties it became so extreme that it was constantly the subject of ridicule. During the Civil War, however, it had advantages. An interesting story is told by Miss McClellan of how an unlicensed dog was saved from the hated dog-catcher by the hooped skirt of his mistress, who deftly hid her pet under its protecting spread, nor would the mistress budge an inch until the catcher of canines, tired at last of waiting and unable to coax the animal from his place of refuge, yielded to lengthening shadows and the jeers of a crowd that had gathered, and left the "pooch" and his owner in peace.

Another tale is told of how a market woman during the Civil War entered Camp carrying, under her hooped petticoat, a roll of army cloth, cavalry boots, flannel, cans of meat and a bag of coffee!

The decline of the hoop came in 1865.

We are apt to think of World War II as curtailing our supply of clothing. It was as nothing compared to the years of the Civil War and its aftermath, when common calico sold for $25 a yard. Southern women at this time made dresses of unbleached muslin and trimmed them with dyed gourd seeds. Feather flowers and rooster's plumes graced many a hat.

The black velvet throat band was revived in 1860, sometimes worn with a pendant in the evening.

During the years 1850-1870, the popular "waterfall" hairdress was copied in doll form; as a matter of fact, popular hairdos were usually copied in doll form in any period. But the doll had the advantage of simplicity. Women had to obtain the effect by using a frame of horsehair attached to the back of the head to form an armature for the hair, which was brushed smoothly over the frame, the ends caught up underneath. Doll heads of the period often, but not always, show the net which was usually worn over the "chignon" or "waterfall." A collector is fortunate to have a doll with this hairdress, either with or without the net, for it is rare. Even the gold color of the net was copied in this miniature way.

It may be interesting to any collector who has the doll with the curl in the middle of the forehead to note that "Miss Reed (of Tennessee) was the original girl with a curl in the middle of her forehead," and that when she introduced the style, it became immediately popular.

Helpful suggestions for costume are found in the quaint illustrations in many magazines of the past. "Harper's New Monthly Magazine" is especially rich in this respect. Sketches 36 and 37 are based on illustrations from "Harper's," 1861. No. 36 (two costumes) is described as the "Home Toilette. the elegance and simplicity of which will commend them to favor. The fullness of detail in the illustrations precludes the necessity of verbal description." The trimming in the sketches has been somewhat simplified, making it a little less difficult to copy in miniature. No. 37 represents a "Spring Pardessus," and a "Spring Pelisse."

No. 38 shows a "Promenade and Dinner Toilette." Figure 1 is a "Promenade Robe" for October, 1864. It is "of light stone-colored merino, with mazarine blue taffeta forming the ornament. This is outlined by a narrow black

36. Two Styles for "Home Toilette." "Harper's," 1861.

38. "Promenade and Dinner Toilette." 1864.

37. "Spring Pardessus" (left) and "Spring Pelisse," 1861.

39. Fig. 1. Bathing Suits of the Civil War Era.
Fig. 2. Mrs. Bloomer, 1850. From an Old Sketch.

velvet, which has an edging of black lace. The robe is made en soutane, that is, the body and skirt are cut in one piece, without seam at the waist."

Figures 2 and 3 are (left), a "Dinner Toilette" and (right) a "Promenade Costume." "The Dinner Toilette is made of mauve taffeta. The corsage is half-high, round waist, revers front, with a frill of Valenciennes lace. Madonna fichu, closed in front by small gold buttons. The Valenciennes is continued from the waist, waved down the front of the skirt; a passementerie of black rosettes is placed at each folding of the lace. The sleeves, which are laid in plaits, are banded in four divisions; with frills of lace, en suite, forming cuffs. As every lady of taste consults that style of coiffure which is individually most becoming to her countenance, we do not think it necessary to specify any special mode.''

Figure 39 illustrates bathing suits of the Civil War era. Louisa M. Alcott's "Little Women" might have worn these outfits.

Figures 40-43 show wearing apparel pictured in "Peterson's Magazine" for 1868. No. 40 is a Carmago mantle; 41, a white "body;" 42, "body;" 43, a black

40-43. **Wearing apparel illustrated in "Peterson's Magazine," 1868.**

silk gored apron; the latter is described as "A very pretty pattern for an apron, to be made of black silk, and gored. At appropriate times, nothing looks so well, on a lady, as a handsome black silk apron."

Figure 44 pictures the costume worn by Clara Barton, founder of the American Red Cross, during the Civil War.

One of the many articles of dress introduced by Eugenie was the "Empress peplin" (1866), a belt with basque tails cut square in front and back and very long at the sides.

Eugenie had such influence on styles that verses were written on the subject. One such reads:

"All women take the fashions

Of Empress and Queen;

Victoria wears the petticoat,

And crinoline—Eugene."

Dolls, of course, copied the "Eugenie" hairdress. Eugenie also sponsored the hair net or snood.

Silk that we still use, the "Foulard," first appeared in 1860. Among the newest designs of that period were pansies, clusters of berries, the cherry and the plum.

Bonnets were flatter on top and wider at the ears than formerly, and hats were small.

Many an old doll of the seventies or eighties has been found with the original basque, a bodice with short skirt or tails below the waist-line, introduced in 1850. Sometimes the tails were long at the rear, sometimes quite short; velvet was the most popular material, worn with silk skirts of contrasting material.

By 1870, dress improvers, or bustles, finally ousted the crinoline. This was the period of the overdress, looped up with bows and rosettes; high bodices and

44. Nurse's Costume, 1862.

sashes; long trains for evening wear, but ankle-length costumes for the street; and small, flat headgear.

Black was worn a great deal, traceable possibly to France, which, in 1870, had troublous times, when "Fashion veiled her face."

Hair, at this period, (1869-70), was worn in braids pinned up at the back, the front hair parted in the middle, waved and drawn back above the ears and ending on top of the head in finger puffs. Curls were fashionable, sometimes a single ringlet hanging down, from the braids over the left shoulder; again, a cluster of small ringlets over the braids. Finger puffs interspersed with artificial flowers were popular for evening wear; and for the street, bonnets reigned supreme.

A very fine source of information on the subject of old costume is the nineteenth century "Delineator." No. 45, Figures 1 and 2, represent Pattern No. 3693 in "The Delineator" for July, 1875, and are described as follows: "Ladies' Costume. Figure No. 1.—The costume delineated on this figure is composed of garments so graceful in every detail as to be independent of elaborate decorations, so that elegant simplicity is its predominating characteristic. The material so stylishly embodied is Sicilienne, and it is prettily relieved from sameness by the scanty arrangement of velvet constituting the decorations. The skirt is in medium train style and hangs in the prevailing mode, with all the fullness retained at the back by the employment of a skirt-adjustor. No trimming, save a large bow tacked at the center of the front, is employed, and hence the lines of the garment, clinging in soft folds to the figure, are at once artistic and fashionable. The graceful over-skirt overlaps at the closing, and then slopes away, forming a V-shaped opening in which the bow comprising the skirt-trimming is placed. The sides are slightly draped by upward-turning plaits, and the looping is the result of tapes beneath. . . .

Fig. 1. Street Costume.   Fig. 2. A Variation of Fig. 1, Back View.

45. Costume of 1875.

"Basques with long side-tabs, such as belong to the garment finishing this costume, are eminently stylish and are used for the dressiest occasions. The basque represented displays a V-shaped opening at the center of the front and under each arm; this fact, together with the deep tabs already alluded to, and the plaited postilion, rendering the garment a truly novel affair. The usual adjusting seams produce the handsome shaping, and a pocket with a tiny lap ornaments each side of the front, while a deep, kilted flounce, below a curved cuff, completes the sleeve, and a full fraise encircles the Vandyke-shaped neck. This costume is susceptible of any amount of trimming, is also available for silk or worsted goods and can be adopted for a variety of occasions. A back view of

Suggestions for Nineteenth Century Doll Costumes

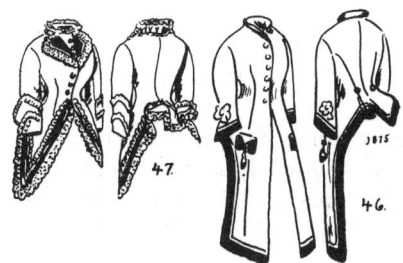

46. Ladies' Demi-Polonaise, 1875.
47. Ladies' Pointed Postilion Basque, 1875.

48. "Lulu," a Cut-out from a Magazine of the 1870's Labelled by a Childish Hand.
49. Another "Paper Doll" Cut-out.

the same costume, made of different materials and with other decorations, may be seen at figure 2."

Evidently the same pattern was used for both figures, although Figure 2 looks very different.

No. 46 shows a "Ladies' Demi-Polonaise" for March, 1875. It is described as an "elegant garment made of silk serge and can be used to complete a suit of the same or other material, but in either event the skirt worn beneath would be extremely stylish if highly ornamented at the back."

No. 47 is a "Ladies' Pointed Postilion Basque" of the same period. To quote, "This stylish affair is made of silk and designed to complete a dinner costume having no over-skirt, the deficiency being amply provided for by the elaborate skirt-trimming."

50. Paper Doll and Costume of the 1870's.

Nos. 48 (name Lulu inscribed on the back by a childish hand) and 49 are cut-outs used as paper dolls by a little girl of the 1870's. One would need to simplify them for real doll costumes. No. 50 was copied from a bona fide paper doll of the late 1870's. It shows the underwear and evening shoes, as well as a hairdo of the day. The costume for the doll, is a beautiful shade of red with an under skirt of background white in a design of red roses. White lace trims bodice and skirts. Old paper dolls, when dated, are fascinating sources of information on costumes of the past.

No. 51 (1-5) shows styles of hats in 1875 and 1884. No. 1 was made to match a costume. No. 2 is described as a simple hat, attractive and elegant. No. 3 is a bonnet made over a frame, and is of velvet with a silk binding. "A roseatte of loops is arranged for the bird." ("The bird on Nellie's hat" was a

Suggestions for Nineteenth Century Doll Costumes

51. Headgear for 1875 and 1884.
1. Hat to Match Costume, 1875.
2. "Simple Hat," 1875.
3. "Velvet Bonnet," 1875.
4. Ladies' Bonnet, 1884.
5. Ladies' "Velvet Poke," 1884.

52-54. Dresses for Paper Doll Cut-outs of 1888.

familiar sight in 1875.) Nos. 4 and 5 (1884) are, respectively, "A Ladies' Poke Bonnet," and a "Velvet Poke."

In 1880, and for a few years thereafter, the bustle disappeared, and loops in a skirt were lowered, but the complicated clumsy skirt, which gave the appearance of window drapery, still persisted throughout the 1880's; there was not much change from the 1870's. Figures 52-54, a child's paper doll cut-outs of 1888, show how unattractive styles were at this time. The bustle at its ugliest had returned. It was the period of tight sleeves and "frizzy" bangs. Scotch plaids and woolen materials were popular, and little hats adorned with plumes, artificial flowers or stuffed birds perched over the bun on top of the head. However, some of the hats were "cute." No. 53 (1 and 2) are, respectively, a bonnet for January, 1884, and a velvet poke for October of the same year. But on the whole, costume was perhaps at its all-time "low." Only a clever artist could put "umph" into such clothes. A Jeanette MacDonald might manage it.

The early nineties saw the revival of the "leg-o'-mutton" sleeve of 1830, and waists were tiny but not as high as in the 1830's. Skirts were much plainer than in the previous decade, and not quite so trailing.

Anyone who collects old paper dolls should have a great variety representing the 1895 period of costume. In that year paper dolls depicting every conceivable style of the times flooded the market. Raphael Tuck & Sons Company of England turned out paper dolls by the millions. These were handsomely colored and beautifully printed. We, in this country, were not far behind. A great many paper dolls were given away with various products. During 1895 and 1896 "The Boston Sunday Herald" issued a "Weekly Colored Costume Plate" with the notation that "duplicate of the 'Model Figure'" will be mailed to subscribers of "The Boston Sunday Herald" upon receipt of four cents (two 2 cent stamps) to cover postage and mailing expenses."

Four of these costumes are pictured here. No. 55 illustrates a "Ladies' Street Toilette, with Marie Antoinette Fur Set." It is of plain grey with ermine cape and muff. Buttons trim the two side pleats, and, the back of the skirt is pleated. This outfit appeared with the October 20, 1895 issue of the paper.

No. 56, "Ladies' Demi-evening Toilette" for February 23, 1896, is typical of the period, when revers, peplum and the plain wide skirt were worn a great deal. The waist has a cream-colored background with a print of rose clusters and foliage. The plain wide skirt matches the foliage in color.

No. 57 represents a white bridal dress with panel of lace at the front of the skirt and a frill of lace down the front of the bodice. It was a cut-out from the set, and the veil was missing. One can get an idea of what it was like by No. 59-a, which represents a bridal costume of about the same period.

No. 58, a "Garden Party Toilette," of 1895 shows an astonishing sunshade—all ruffles—and made of the same material as the dress, which seems to be a corded figured white silk. A blue pointed lace collar and blue ribbon at the waist add a touch of color. The hat accompanying the costume is a garden of pink roses atop an undulating frame festooned with a fringed edge.

A whole set of these Sunday supplements would make an interesting booklet to illustrate 1895-1896 women's costumes. Nothing seems to have been omitted.

Suggestions for Nineteenth Century Doll Costumes

55. Ladies' "Street Toilette," 1895.
56. Ladies' "Demi-evening Toilette," 1896.

57. White Bridal Dress, 1895 or 1896.
58. "Garden Party Toilette," 1895.

Even sports outfits—tennis, horseback riding, bicycling and swimming—were included. Some of them must have been considered quite daring for 1895. Tennis and cycling costumes cleared ground to the shoe tops, and bathing costumes (my dears!) exposed at least the shape of the leg to the knee, although discreetly covered with "blackout" stockings. The sporting man and woman of those days must have made quite a pair. The sporting gentleman wore "Norfolk Jacket" and knickerbockers.

59. A Bride and Her Outfit circa 1900. (Paper doll.)

All through the last decade of the century women wore the high neck and long sleeve. Toward its close came a revival of the "Garibaldi" blouse, although the color was not restricted to red, the popular color of earlier years. As a climax to ugly style during the closing years of the century, the "kangaroo" shape for women threw hips back and the bust forward by especially designed corsets; and long trains gathered up dust from the streets. By about 1900 sleeves were not quite so exaggerated as they had been, and attention was given to fine underwear. Sketch 59 shows a paper doll bride and her outfit at this time.

We leave costume for adults in the late nineteenth century with a sigh of relief and with the hope that those who have some of the really beautiful dolls of the later years dress them conservatively.

Chapter VIII

Children's Clothes in the Nineteenth Century

EARLY nineteenth century children's dresses continued, as in previous centuries, to be miniature copies of their elders. However, the simplicity of style was suitable for youngsters, except that girls wore dresses too long for convenience. This was the era that Kate Greenaway made popular toward the close of the century. Sketches 60 (a boy of 1806) and 61 (a girl of 1813) are typical. About 1813 pantalettes came in, although they were not in general use until later. They hampered the freedom of the newly developed shorter skirt for girls.

60. A Boy of 1806.
61. A Girl of 1813.

62. A Child's Dress of 1828. (From a contemporary picture of Princess Victoria.)

While the plain ones were not difficult to wear, the beruffled fancies must have been a heartache to all but the most vain.

Sketch No. 62, taken from a picture of Princess (later Queen) Victoria of England when she was nine years of age, does not show pantalettes, which were especially popular at that time. But this was a "party" dress, therefore long. Notice that the hair in the picture is short; two years later Victoria again had her portrait painted, this time with ringlets.

Sketch No. 63 shows a dress for a six-year-old with plain pantalettes showing. It was taken from an unsigned painting of 1833.

No. 64 shows an early doll in original dress. The body is like an adult, but the costume is that of a young girl.

It would be interesting to dress a boy and a girl doll as in sketch No. 65. These quaint styles for children fascinate old and young alike.

63. Dress for a Six-year-old Girl. (From an unsigned painting dated 1833.)

64. Doll in Original Costume, circa 1830.

65. Costume for Girl, 1835; Boy, 1840.

Except in the matter of skirt length, fashions for girls until the late nineteenth century were usually only slightly simplified versions of their elders, although they were charming during the first part of the 1800's. Children did not wear stiff corsets as in previous centuries, when even two-year-olds were encased in that harmful item of wearing apparel, but suitable simplicity was not the dominant note after about 1840.

Sketch No. 66 shows Princess Victoria again, this time a young lady of sixteen. Notice the plain gown. The Princess's mother was noted for her good sense in dressing Victoria. While the hairdo (used for many old dolls of the period) represents a "grown-up" it must be remembered that in those days a girl who had passed her fifteenth birthday was expected to dress like a fully grown woman. A study of patterns for this period and later in the Library of Congress, Washington, D. C., has revealed no "misses" costumes for the girl older than fifteen. They usually read "Children—six months to six years;" "Girls—five to eight" or "three to nine;" "Misses—eight to fifteen." Of course there are variations.

The eighteen forties saw little country girls with sunbonnets of calico stiffened with rows of cording. Low half-bodices over guimpes of white muslin, and full skirts stiffened with crinoline were quite the thing, and, between 1835 and 1870, gaiter boots. Almost all the china-legged dolls of this period boasted gaiter boots. Sleeves to the elbow were introduced in 1840, and have remained more or less in style ever since.

White was the favorite color for little girls throughout the nineteenth century. During the eighteen fifties, rows of embroidered insertion gladdened

66. Costume for a Young Girl, 1835. (After the painting of Princess Victoria by Sir George Hayter.)

the hearts of the very young. Bonnets were fashionable, but hats, too, were worn. In the eighteen sixties hats for girls under ten years of age were called "flats." They might better have been called "flappers" because of the wide, flapping brims.

In 1800 girls wore their hair cut short, but soon afterward curls came into vogue. Up to 1835, hair was parted in the middle. Between that year and 1870, two pigtails worn down the back was a popular style. Another style introduced in 1840 was the back-comb arrangement. The hair was brushed off the forehead with no part showing, a style which continued in favor during the remainder of the century and later. "Child" dolls as well as "grown-ups" of the "covered wagon" era often show this hairdo. If a doll represented an older girl or a lady, the back hair might be encased in a net.

Sketch No. 67 shows a China "young girl" of the 1850's and a side view of the back-comb. Her black cotton dress with floral design is trimmed with fine net ruching, undersleeves and fichu of white batiste. She wears the typical china gaiter flat-soled boots of the pre-Civil War doll.

"Boy" dolls of this period followed the custom of parting the hair very much to one side. In the 1860's, boys as well as girls usually parted the hair directly in the middle. Later in the century the boys distinguished themselves

67. China "Young Girl" of the 1850's.

by again parting the hair at the side, the older boys cropping their hair closer to the head than in the early years.

No. 68 (1-7) shows a group of children's clothes from 1850 to 1862. No. 1 represents a boy's costume (1862) of light drab cloth decorated with black braid.

Nos. 2 and 3 represent, respectively, a girl and a boy of 1861. No. 3 has been graduated to bloomers under his skirt; hence an older child than No. 1.

No. 4 is a child's dress of 1860.

No. 5 is described as "a pleasing style of dress for a little boy. A Charles-the-Ninth cap of black velvet with a well-rolled feather on one side, and proceeding from a cabbage-rose of black satin ribbon. Coat of black velvet, without any seam at the waist. It is hollowed out at the side and back seams, like a lady's paletot, tight over the breast, and fastened with little jet buttons. Sleeves half short, also with buttons. Under the coat is a tunic of plaid poplin, black and red. This tunic is full of gathers like a Scottish kilt. Plaid stockings, stripes sloping; small black gaiters with jet buttons. Collar sewed onto a band; the trimmings of the under-sleeves and trousers are of the older style of English embroidery."

Children's Clothes in the Nineteenth Century 75

68. Children's Clothes from 1850 to 1862.

No. 1. Boy's Costume of 1862.
No. 2. A girl of 1861.
No. 3. A Boy's Bloomer-and-skirt Costume.
No. 4. A Child's Dress of 1860.
No. 5. "A Pleasing Style of Dress for a Little Boy."
No. 6. "An Elegant Costume for a Little Girl."
No. 7. "A Neat Costume for a Little Girl." (1850.)

Figure 6 (1851) represents "an elegant costume for a little girl, three or four years of age—a pretty, fair-haired creature. The frock is of white silk, embroidered sky blue, body low and square in front, with two silk lapels, embroidered and festooned; a frill along the top of the front, with an embroidered insertion below it. The sleeves are embroidered; a broad blue ribbon passes between the shoulder and the sleeve, and is fastened at top by a rosette with loose ends. This manner of tying the ribbon raises the sleeve and leaves the arm uncovered at top. The skirt is composed of two insertions and two embroidered flounces. An embroidered petticoat reaches below the skirt. The sash is of blue silk and very wide."

Figure 7 (1850) is described as "a neat costume for a little girl. Dress of glacé silk, shaded in light green and lilac. The skirt trimmed with four rows of fringe of green and lilac silk intermingled. The corsage low and plain, with a pelerine which passes along the back and shoulders, and is brought down to the front of the waist in a point. This pelerine is edged with two rows of fringe. The sleeves of the dress, which are short, are edged simply with one row of fringe. Attached to these short sleeves are long sleeves of white muslin made so as to set nearly close to the upper part of the arms, but finished between the elbow and the wrist with three drawings separated by bands of needlework in-

69. Children's Costumes from 1861-1863.
   No. 1. A Street Dress of 1862.
   No. 2. A Boy and Girl of 1863.
   No. 3. Child's Street Dress, 1863.
   No. 4. Girl's Light Drab Pardessus.
   No. 5. Boy's Costume, 1862.

sertion. Above these drawings there is a frill which falls back on the arm. The neck is covered by a chemisete of muslin, finished at the throat with a trimming of needlework, turned over."

No. 69, sketches 1-5, represent children's costumes of 1861 to 1863. No. 1, the little girl with the hoop, wears a street dress of 1862. In this we see the influence of the bloomer costume and ruffles of the 1850 period still in vogue.

No. 2 shows a boy and girl of 1863. The girl's dress (figure on left) is described as follows: "The bodice is of black velvet, à la Suisse, over a chemisette of Nansouk. The skirt is of Mexican-blue foulard."

The boy is described as having a jacket of green velvet with a vest of salmon colored merino, and an embroidered skirt of the same material. There was no indication in the sketch which accompanied this description of embroidery in the pleated skirt, but, evidently, there was embroidery down the front of the jacket. It is difficult for moderns to realize that this outfit is for a small boy. Even the hair arrangement is girlish. If one dressed a doll of the 1860's in this ensemble, it would certainly be taken for a girl—a very charming little girl.

70. Child with Mother.

No. 3 gives us only the back of an 1863 "child's street dress" but it is evident that this is perfectly plain, trimmed only by two bands of contrasting material around the bottom of the skirt, and a sash around the waist.

No. 4 is described as a girl's light drab Pardessus, the date, 1862.

No. 5 is a boy's costume "believe it or not," for December, 1862. No description is given of the material used except that it is "adapted to almost any of the seasonable materials."

All the costumes in Nos. 68 and 69 were taken from early copies of "Harper's New Monthly Magazine." All are for small children; otherwise the sketches would show heeled shoes, which reappeared in Europe in 1860, as stated before.

Sketch No. 70 ("Harper's" 1864) is reproduced to show the interesting child's dress. It is described as being made of worsted, ornamented with embroidery and braid.

Sketches numbered 71 and 72 are adapted from styles in Godey's "Lady's Book and Magazine," 1867. No. 71, sketch 1 is a child's dress of white piqué braided with scarlet braid. "This same pattern is suited admirably to wool materials." No. 2 is a child's Pelisse of muslin with embroidered frills headed by bouillonnées. The buttons and ceinture are of silk. No. 2-a is a "Muslin Body, the under portion in tucks crossed with narrow velvet from the neck to the waist. The jacket is of plain muslin trimmed with embroidery. The undersleeves are ornamented with blue taffeta ribbons and small buttons.'' Pattern dated August, 1864.

No. 3 is described as a dress for a child just putting on short clothes. "This little dress may be made of white cambric or piqué, trimmed with bands of

71. **Children's Dresses from Styles in "Godey's Lady's Book and Magazine," 1867.**

No. 1. Child's Dress of White Pique.

No. 2. Child's Pelisse; 2-a, Muslin Body.

No. 3. "Dress for a Child Just Putting on Short Clothes."

No. 4. Alpaca Dress for a Little Girl."

colored cambric stitched down each side in a pattern. The yoke is formed of colored cambric trimmed with Cluny lace."

No. 4 is an alpaca dress for a little girl and is dated January, 1867. "It is made square in the neck, and finished on the edge of the skirt and corsage by scallops bound with velvet."

No. 72 shows eight ways of trimming children's dresses of 1867.

Early copies of "Peterson's Magazine" often show the actual pattern for clothes illustrated and described. No. 73 is "The Parisian Costume" for 1868, and is described as follows: "The pretty costume is very fashionable at the present time among French boys from four to six years of age. It is usually made of black velvet and decorated with jet buttons. The knickerbockers match the overcoat, and the under-dress consists of either scarlet or blue silk. The stockings and belt match the underdress in color.

"Our diagram represents exactly one-half of the over-dress, viz:

    No. 1. Half of Front.
    No. 2. Half of Back.
    No. 3. Half of Skirt of Back.

"The fronts are cut double-breasted, and fasten from the shoulder downward. The opening is at the right side. A notch will be found at the neck where

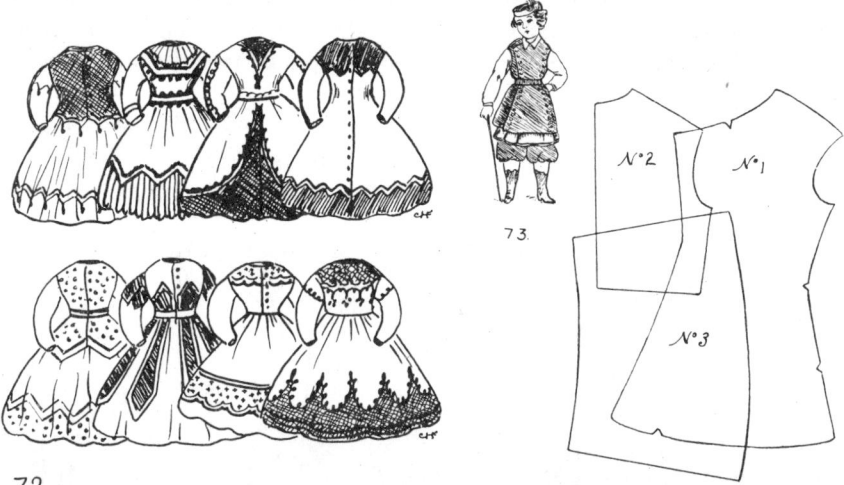

72. Eight Ways of Trimming Children's Dresses of 1867.

73. Parisian Costume for 1868, with Pattern.

the revers cross. The notch at the bottom marks the center of the front. The back is in two pieces—the top and the skirt. The latter is plaited at the waist, and the notch at the one side marks the openings for the pocket-hole.

"This costume also looks well in either blue or scarlet cashmere or reps, with white beneath. The under-dress is merely a high petticoat, with long sleeves."

Pattern 74-a ("Peterson's," 1868) has been adapted for a china-headed doll (74) of about the same period. It is called a "Basquine for a Little Girl" and the numbers in the pattern are as follows:

        No. 1, Half the Front.   No. 4, Half the Collar.
        No. 2, Half the Back.   No. 5, Half the Sleeve.
        No. 3, Half the Cape.   No. 6, Half the Cuff.

Patterns designed especially for dolls' clothes seem to have started with "The Delineator" in February, 1875. The following is quoted from their "Dolls' Department" for that year:

"In articles with the above heading, we propose furnishing our little girl readers with instructions which will be of service to them in taking care of and preparing the wardrobes of their dollies. We shall also publish in these articles styles for dolls' garments, for which we shall have patterns put up in sets and enclosed in envelopes, accompanied by very simple directions for making them. There will be different sizes of them for dolls from twelve to twenty-four inches in length, so that you can get a pattern to fit dolly, but it would be best to take her measure first and then select a pattern.

"Set No. 1 consists of a chemise, pair of drawers and a night-dress with a yoke; the price of the entire set is only ten cents . . . . . .

"The little night-dress has a yoke and is open in front, and is just as near like those worn by grown-up ladies as can be. The drawers are open at one side, and the chemise is cut in two pieces, the sleeves lapping at the top under tiny pearl buttons."

In the issues of the magazine which followed were patterns for dolls showing different age groups—baby dolls, grown-ups and the nearly grown. No. 2 is a "child" doll dressed as a "lady." Others pictured grown-up proportions, such

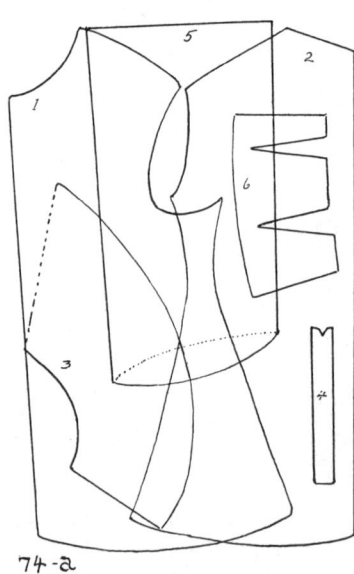

74. China-headed Doll in Basquine Dress, Pattern for which was taken from "Peterson's Magazine" for 1868.

74-a. Pattern for Basquine.

as in Set No. 3, consisting of a "walking skirt and yoke waist." The latter appeared in the January, 1884 issue of "The Delineator," and was entitled "Lady Doll's Toilette." No. 4 appeared in the same issue under the heading, "Girl Doll's Set . . . .Walking Skirt and Breton Jacket."

We do not often find an antique doll in original costume that is at all presentable. No. 76 is one of the exceptions to the rule. It is made of fine brown woolen material, and trimmed with bands of narrow black velvet ribbon. The doll and costume are typical of the early 1860's. No. 77, a tiny one, is said on good authority to have been a doll belonging to Abraham Lincoln's aunt. It is in original dress.

Children's Clothes in the Nineteenth Century

75. "Dolls' Department." ("The Delineator," 1875.)

    No. 1. Chemise, pair of drawers, nightdress.

    No. 2. Doll's Dress.

    No. 3. Walking Skirt and Yoke Waist. ("The Delineator," 1884.)

    No. 4. Walking Skirt and Breton Jacket (1884.)

76. China-headed Doll in Original Costume, Civil War Period.

77. Tiny China-headed Doll in Original Dress, said to have belonged to an aunt of Abraham Lincoln.

Dolls in Sketch No. 78 appeared as "visiting dolls" in a book called "De Deux Poupees," Paris, 1864. At the left is Gracieuse, a French doll; at the right, Roselein, a German beauty.

No. 79 are also "visiting dolls" from the same publication. In the center

78. "Visiting Dolls," Gracieuse and Roselein, Sketched from "De Deux Poupees," Paris, 1864.

79. "Visiting Dolls," Miss Darling, Nina, Panna Minutka.

is Nina, a Spanish "ballet dancer;" to the left of her is Miss Darling, an English "girl;" at the right, Panna Minutka, a Polish doll.

No. 80 (Carol) is a china-headed doll dressed in the latest 1875 costume. The skirt is an accordion-pleated affair, made from a bell-shaped light blue silk sleeve of long ago (which was conveniently so pleated) and a dark blue velvet basque trimmed with braid. An under waist is of thin white batiste.

80. Carol, a China-headed Doll in Dress of 1875.

81. Dickie, a China-headed Doll of 1875.

No. 81 (Dickie), representing a boy's costume of the same year, is brother to Carol. His jacket is also of dark blue velvet, his trousers olive-drab, and his small vest is made from a white kid glove. Collar and cuffs came from a nineteenth century ladies' petticoat.

Nos. 82 (Rebecca) and 83 (James) form another brother-sister combination, for they were "born" at about the same time, circa 1880. Sailor blouses, knickerbockers and striped stockings were worn by a great many little boys in the late nineteenth century. Rebecca's dress is original. It is pink trimmed with white ruffles and braid.

No. 84, "Pinkie," is a stone bisque-headed "bonnet doll" of the Kate Greenaway period. The bonnet, moulded on, is shaded in pink, and her pink dress is trimmed with lace and insertion. No. 85 is a "bonnet" head in china in shades of brown, white and yellow. The latter is of the same general period as "Pinkie."

No. 86 is the original infant's dress which came on a wax doll formerly belonging in the family of the famous preacher, Henry Ward Beecher, brother of the equally famous Harriet Beecher Stowe, author of "Uncle Tom's Cabin." The dress, with its dainty embroidery and lace edging, is yellow with age, but completely intact. The doll (Harriet) came to its present owner, Claire Fawcett,

82. Rebecca, a China-headed Doll of 1880.

83. James, a China-headed Doll Circa 1880.

85. A "Bonnet" Head of China.

84. Pinkie, a Bisque-headed "Bonnet" Doll circa 1885.

via the auction room when the effects of a Beecher descendant were put "on the block."

Another charming little nineteenth century baby dress belongs to Mrs. Luta E. Ferrell of Washington, D. C. This is No. 87. A detail from the embroidered flounce of the dress (87-a) is also shown.

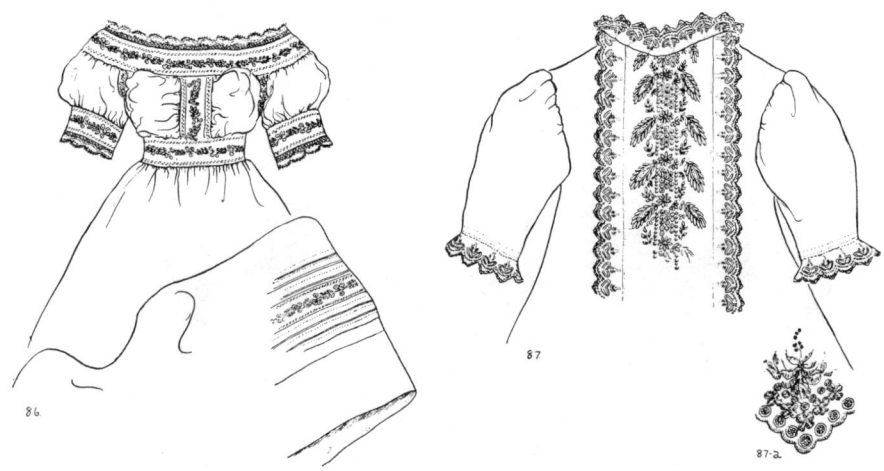

86. Infant Doll Dress Formerly Owned by the Children of Henry Ward Beecher.

87. Nineteenth Century Infant's Dress Owned by Mrs. Luta E. Ferrell of Washington, D. C.
a. Detail from Embroidered Flounce.

No. 88 is an over-dress which came with an old doll of the 1880's. It is made like the "Gabrielle" described in "The Story of Alice and Mabel" except that it is looped up at the side and tied with a bow of plain material.

Compare No. 89, "Costume for a Girl, 5-12, for October, 1885" with No. 90. a boy's costume for July, 1875. The style is similar, except that the girl has a plain skirt and fancy yoke, while the boy's skirt is pleated, he has a plain bodice, and the bow at the back is slightly smaller.

No. 91 appeared in the May issue of "The Delineator" for 1885. It is called a "Misses Polonaise Costume."

No. 92, a and b shows what the big girl of fifteen might be expected to wear in 1885, a was designed for winter wear, b for the summer. An elaborate description comes with a, which illustrates a Princess dress for misses eight to fifteen years of age. To quote:

"Two fabrics—plain and embroidered cashmere—are most attractively combined in this instance. The Princess is beautifully fitted by single bust and under-arm darts and gracefully shaped side-back gores. It is closed at the back with button-holes and buttons to a desirable distance below the waist-line, and below the closing the skirt is cut on a fold of the goods, the extra width at the center being under-folded in a box-plait. The front is seamless at the center, and upon it is arranged a beautiful round drapery, that is closely plaited up at its back edges and sewed to position at these and its upper edges, the center drooping in graceful folds and the back edges extending to the side-back seams. The back-drapery is stylishly puffy and presents the bow effect at the top. It is folded and seamed across the top, and is shirred along and at each side of the seam, the shirrings being drawn up closely and secured to a stay placed under them. The sides of the drapery are widely hemmed, and two deep loops are

88. Over-dress on a Doll's Costume of 1880.

tacked in the hems, the upper loops producing the bow effect. At these loops the drapery is tacked to the dress, while its center is caught to the body at the closing with a hook and loop. Both draperies are of the embroidered goods and are finished plainly. A box-plaited flounce of the plain goods, headed by two rows of soutache braid, trims the bottom of the dress prettily. A row of the braid overlies the officer's collar at the neck and outlines round cuffs at the wrists of the coat sleeves. Ruffs of crêpe lisse are worn in the neck and sleeves.

"Any preferred combination of materials may be selected for dresses of this style, and the trimming on the skirt may be plaitings, ruffles, ruches, wide contrasting bands, braids, etc., as most pleasing to the taste and best suited to the goods chosen. Silks, velvets, velveteens, cashmeres, satins, camel's-hairs and all varieties of woolen dress goods, in plaited, striped or figured patterns or plain colors, are adapted to the mode and may be used singly or in combinations of two or three, velvet combining stylishly with almost all textures. Cashmere, nun's

89. Costume for a Girl, 1885.
90. Costume for a Boy, 1875.
91. Misses' Polonaise Costume.
92. Costume for a Fifteen-year-old, 1885.

veiling, China silk and Surah are charming for misses' evening dresses, and may be found in all the evening tints. Lace is added lavishly to evening costumes, and sometimes the draperies are of lace net.''

Aprons were very much used in earlier days, especially during the period when elaborate and costly clothes were worn. The average person owned far fewer clothes than the woman or child of today, and the wear and tear on them necessitated protection. In most families the girl of twelve was allowed one clean print dress and two aprons a week. Bed was considered the proper place for her if she couldn't make this generous (?) allowance do. For summer wear, aprons were low-necked and short-sleeved; winter aprons were more like dresses. In fact, they were often used as dresses in the summer time.

No. 93 is described as follows: "An apron, made of cambric and trimmed with a bias band of the same and a ruffle of embroidery, shirred at the waist-line and arranged between two side-gores; while the back is similarly shirred and has side-seams. The latter are discontinued beneath the belt. In place of sleeves, pointed shoulder-straps are fastened at the top of the apron under pearl buttons. Similar buttons are in the upper corners of the pockets ornamenting the front. The graceful outline of the skirt is prettily set off by the ruffle of embroidery and band of material arranged about the margin, a decoration which completes all the remaining edges of the garment. The apron is closed with buttons at the back . . . .

"The pattern is in eight sizes for misses from eight to fifteen years of age."

This apron, and No. 94, an apron for a child two to six years of age, appeared in the July, 1875, issue of "The Delineator."

No. 95 is described (1885) as "a Mother Hubbard apron for a two- to twelve-year-old." This style lasted until the twentieth century. We wonder how many 50-year-olds of today remember the "Mother Hubbard" apron of their childhood. No. 96, made very plainly, is for a tot six months to three years old; Nos. 97 and 98 for a girl three to nine years of age. No. 99, a "Pompadour," and No. 100, a "low-necked apron" are for the 3 to 12-year-olds. And No. 101 is described as a "Misses' Sack Apron" for the eight to fifteen-year-old. This is a winter apron worn as a dress in the summer time. The sketch (No. 102) of the apron-clad child and her doll and carriage was clipped from a magazine by a little girl of long ago. All the aprons described in this paragraph are of the 1885 vintage. No. 103 is a sketch of an original doll's apron of the late nineteenth century. The design is a black print on a white background.

Infants at this time wore long, full, elaborately trimmed dresses, often with a huge bow of self-material tied at the back. The bow strings were sewn into the seam directly under the arm-pit. Babies' outfits, with their tucks and ruffles and dainty embroidery and lace, which have survived the years, are monuments to the patient endurance of mothers and grandmothers and fond "aunties." On some of the garments there are as many as twenty-four tucks sewn by hand with the tiniest stitches imaginable, all round a voluminous skirt. Material used in one wee baby's garment at that period would make a dress for a grown-up in more recent times. Sketch 104 shows one of the more conservative baby dresses of 1884. Infant christening robes were gorgeous creations, some with panels of exquisite embroidery and lace.

Children's Clothes in the Nineteenth Century

93. Cambric Apron with Ruffle of Embroidery for Misses 8-15 years of age, 1875.
94. Apron for a Child 2-6 years of age, 1875.
95. Mother Hubbard Apron, 2-12 years of age, 1885.
96. Apron for Tot 6 months to 3 years old.
97. Apron for Girl 3-9 years of age.
98. Apron for Girl 3-9 years of age.
99. Pompadour Apron for Girl 3-12 years of age.
100. Low-necked Apron for Girl 3-12 years of age.
101. Misses' Sack Apron, 8-15 years of age.

90   ON MAKING, MENDING AND DRESSING DOLLS

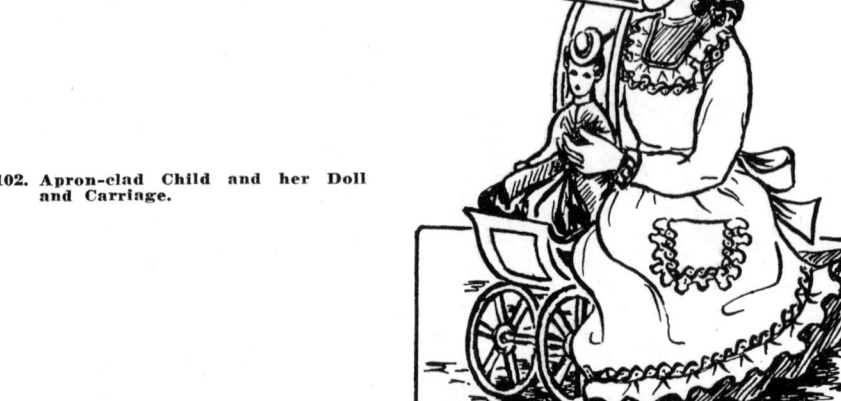

102. Apron-clad Child and her Doll and Carriage.

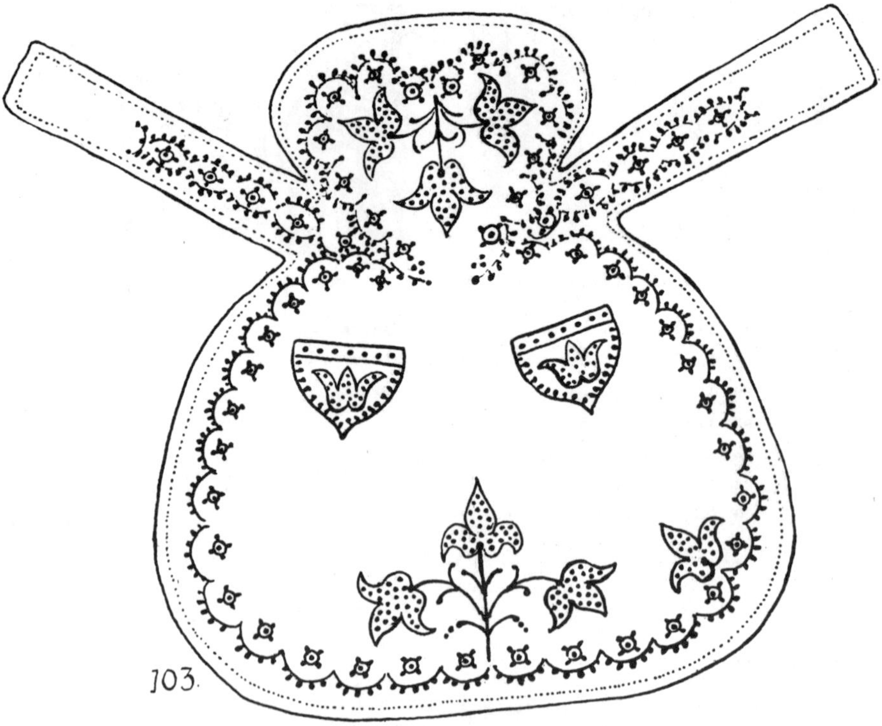

103. Original Doll's Apron of the late Nineteenth Century.

Childrens costumes for the closing years of the century are well exemplified in paper dolls. So many of the latter were made during the eighteen nineties and preserved in later years that we have ample opportunity to study them. Some museums have fine collections.

No. 105 is an English paper doll sold in this country as well as abroad. The original box shows a picture of the doll dressed in costume and hat repro-

104. Infant's Dress of 1884.

105. Raphael Tuck Paper Doll Showing Dress and Hat of 1894.

duced at the right of doll, and reads as follows: "Lady Edith with Dresses and Hats. No. 4 of our Pets. Series of Dressing Dolls. Designed by Margaret McDonald. Raphael Tuck & Sons Co., Ltd., London, Paris, New York." No date is given, but it seems to be of about the same period as the Tuck Artistic Series of 1894. The doll is dressed (including stockings) in pale grayish lavender, with white ruffle around neck, white ribbon bow, white puff sleeves with ribbon trimming to match dress. Light hair, with red rose at left of bangs. Dress at right is of yellow with indistinct white dots, pansies and ribbon trimming of plum color. Yellow hat trimmed with plum colored ribbon and plumes.

Red rose under hat brim. Tuck dolls came in various sizes. This sketch was taken from an eight-inch doll; No. 106 from a twelve-inch one.

The school outfit which comes with No. 106 is conservative as to sleeve. Most of the sleeves of that period were very wide, even wider than those shown in the "party" dress at the right of the doll. The name Vi is given for convenience. No name could be found on box or clothing of this particular doll.

106. Raphael Tuck Paper Doll Showing Underwear, Dress and Hat of 1894.

Printed on the back of the doll was the following: "R T S Artistic Series (printed on easel or stand of the figure.) Publishers by appointment to Their Majesties The King and Queen Alexandra. Patd. Feb. 20th, 1894. Raphael Tuck and Sons, Ltd., London, Paris, Berlin, New York and Montreal. Designed at the studios in New York and printed at the Fine Arts Works in Saxony."

Vi, who has brown hair and blue eyes—and, incidentally, a head that comes off and fits over an elongated neck on the various costumes—wears the usual white underwear, very fancily trimmed with lavender bows of ribbon. The bows on her slippers are the same shade of lavender. Her stockings are striped in two shades of tan, and she has tan shoes. The "party" dress at right of the doll, is red trimmed with green bow at neck and green sash, and an over-bodice of cream net. She carries red roses to match the roses in her hat. The latter is green with green plumes in a lighter shade. Tan gloves.

The school outfit, No. 107-a, with matching hat, is in blue, and the jumper dress (b) is a green pleated affair, the bodice trimmed with yellow buttons. A lavender bow at the neck finishes off the blouse, which is green with white

Children's Clothes in the Nineteenth Century

107. School Dresses and Hats of 1894.

108. Beach Costume for Doll No. 106.

stripes. Her hat to go with this costume is plum colored velvet with a yellow silk lining to match the plume to the left, the other plume is green. Both are held with a gold buckle.

Vi's beach dress, No. 108, is dark blue trimmed with light blue bands at the bottom and around the collar. The latter is red ending in a red bow matching the stockings. At the neck is a blue bow. Tan slippers with blue ties complete the costume.

Fashion plates of the past are apt to give only one side of the picture—the extreme of fashion. In order to get a clearer vision we must look through other illustrated literature, stories of the lives of average persons in any given time. There were always conservatives in every period.

Some of the ideas in dress which we think of as entirely modern were thought of many years ago. People are not much different now than they were fifty or more years back. In this connection, "Mamma in Miniature" written for "The Puritan" in November, 1899, is interesting:

"One of the transitory whims of fashionable young mothers is to dress small daughters exactly like themselves upon any particular or picturesque occasion. If discreetly done, the effect is quaint and pleasing as well as diverting to the lookers on.

"A maternal beauty often accompanies herself with her own miniature replica to emphasize the charms common to both, and accentuate the notes of a thoughtful toilette by repetition.

"The pose, too, is tender and becoming and conducive to sentimental interest. People say 'Isn't it pretty, the intimacy between Mrs. Blank and her little girl! The child is rarely seen without her. They verily look more like sisters than mother and daughter. The child is just the mother through the other end of an opera glass.' "

One of most interesting dolls of this period, and one which looks most fitting in "Gay Nineties" clothes, is the one designed by Charles Dana Gibson. His pictures of the American Girl have immortalized the costume of the young woman of the closing years of the nineteenth century, and of the beginning of the twentieth century.

Chapter IX

On Dressing the "Period" Doll

MANY persons prefer dressing dolls according to periods or persons in history regardless of when the doll itself was made. This is especially true of the teacher who is a collector. History is personalized when a doll representing the period is presented to the student.

Favorite subjects among those who make and costume dolls are "The White House Ladies," to which a chapter in this book is devoted, historic figures, famous artists' models, brides of all times, and the typical garb of any given period or country. Some even go so far as to attempt to trace the whole history of

109. Changing Form of Skirt and Sleeve of the Tunica.

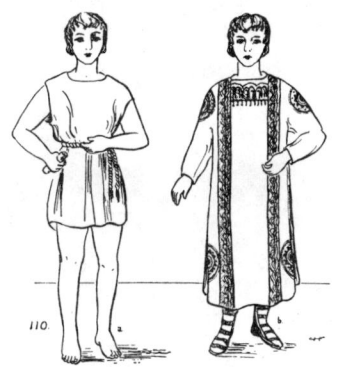

110. a: The Tunica of the Early Greeks and Romans.

b: The Tunica Talaris Worn as an Every-day Garment by the Clergy in the Middle of the Fourth Century.

costume from the first woven articles of clothing—the tunic, the trousers and the cloak—down to the present time. In this chapter are pictured suggestions for "period" costumes.

The changing form of skirt and sleeve of the Tunica of the early Greeks and Romans is shown in sketches No. 109. No. 110-a shows how the tunica was worn, and b, the tunica talaris worn as an every-day garment by the clergy in the middle of the fourth century. Clothes representing this era are simple to make. Moreover, every costume told a story of the wearer; even the decorations particularly had meaning. Garments were definitely part of the history of the times.

The late thirteenth century was an interesting costume period. This was Dante's time, and the figure showing typical attire, No. 111, is worn by his Beatrice. The head in the drawing was taken from an old engraving.

111. Late Thirteenth Century Attire.
(Head from an old engraving of
Dante's Beatrice.)

No. 112 (a-d) shows sixteenth century costume. The central figure is Margaret of France or Valois (1553-1615); a is Elizabeth of Austria (1554-1592); b, Mary Stuart (1542-1587); c, Gabrielle of Estrees (1571-1599); d, Louise of Lorraine (1554-1601).

This was a colorful era for both men's and women's costume. No. 113 (a and b) represent men's clothing for the latter half of the sixteenth century.

No. 114 shows seventeenth century attire. The central figure is Henrietta Anne of England (1644-1670;) 1, Maria Theresa of Austria (1638-1683;) 2, Louis XIV (1638-1715;) 3, Henrietta Maria of England (1609-1669;) 4, Marie de Rohan-Montbason (1600-1679.)

Dorothy W. Heizer, of Essex Falls, N. J., an artist who ranks high in the field of doll making, has given such excellent examples of gowns worn by fam-

112. Sixteenth Century Costume. (After contemporary paintings.) Center, Margaret of France or Valois, 1553-1615.

    a: Elizabeth of Austria, 1554-1592.

    b: Mary Stuart, 1542-1587.

    c: Gabrielle of Estrees, 1571-1599.

    d: Louise of Lorraine, 1554-1601.

ous persons in history that they are a marvel to all beholders. It would be difficult indeed to visualize a finer interpretation of Henry VIII or Marie Antoinette than is to be found in the late Mrs. Frank B. Noyes' collection of dolls by this artist. "Henry" is so perfect in every detail (as are all Miss Heizer's dolls)

113. Men's Costume in the Latter Half of the Sixteenth Century.

that, standing before him, one feels the atmosphere of the old English monarch Even the tiny jewels look like the real things.

Marie Antoinette, copied from a Madame Le Brun painting, stands aloof from this truly remarkable collection in a gilt Italian cabinet lined with blue. Her clothing is taken from pieces of the material the famous queen actually wore. They were offered Mrs. Noyes by the screen star Miss Colleen Moore, who in turn received them from a direct descendant of a lady-in-waiting to the Queen.

Miss Helen Vogt, who wrote the story of this doll for "The Evening Star" of Washington, D. C., had the same feeling as the writer on beholding the miniature Queen. In her words, "To describe the figure would be an injustice to the actual model, for one cannot imagine the beauty of these fine old fabrics—they must be seen. Briefly, however, the doll is dressed in an ornate gown of satin brocade, beautifully worked with hand embroidery of the finest type. The bodice is cut low and edged with the lace which also belonged to Marie Antoinette—as are the elbow-length sleeves and bouffant overskirt. The latter, a continuation of the bodice, meets at the tiny waist and falls away to form a bustle effect and to reveal the lovely blue striped satin skirt in front. The skirt is embroidered in the daintiest needle-work, and the bodice, sleeves and overskirt are made of rich, cream-colored brocaded satin with tiny bouquets of hand embroidered flowers. Accessories take the form of a plum-colored velvet chapeau with plumes and a large bow at the back; slippers of the same shade with enormous buckles and necklace, bracelets and rings which accurately resemble the jewels worn by

114. Seventh Century Attire. (After contemporary paintings.) Center, Henrietta Anne of England, 1644-1670.

1. Maria Theresa of Austria, 1638-1683.
2. Louis XIV, 1638-1715.
3. Henrietta Maria of England, 1609-1669.
4. Marie de Rohan-Montbason, 1600-1679.

this queen. In her hand the doll holds a rose tied with ribbon. The hair is 'blonde poudre.' Enormous and elaborate white wigs were worn only at state functions.''

Some day the whole Noyes collection, including a number of distinctive antique dolls, may be on public display. If they are given a room at the Smith-

115. Marie Antoinette, 1755-1793. Costume Doll by Dorothy Heizer.

116. Louis of Prussia, 1776-1810. Costume Doll by Dorothy Heizer.
117. Empress Josephine of France, 1763-1814. Costume Doll by Dorothy Heizer.

sonian Institution in Washington, D. C., all doll lovers who visit it surely will want to spend some time studying not only the tiny (fourteen-inch) kings, queens and nobles of an earlier day—including the twenty-inch Marie Antoinette—but the "period" dolls representing the common people (at twenty-five-year intervals) from 1775 to 1925. The workmanship is a revelation to

118. Eugenie, Empress of France, 1826-1920. Costume Doll by Dorothy Heizer.

119. Catherine II of Russia, 1729-1796. Costume Doll by Dorothy Heizer.

amateur doll dressers. That such perfection can be worked out in miniature is almost beyond belief.

Five sketches (115-119) of the dolls are reproduced here. They are as follows: Marie Antoinette, 1755-1793; Louise of Prussia, 1776-1810; Empress Josephine, 1763-1814; Eugenie, Empress of France, 1826-1920 and Catherine II of Russia, 1729-1796.

Large museums all over the country have utilized dolls to show "period" costumes. The Metropolitan Museum of Art in New York City has a fine collection of such dolls. These are not always on display, but through the courtesy of the Museum, six of the dolls are reproduced here. They are (No. 120) a, French Costume, 1420-1460; b, French Costume—style worn by Mary, Queen of Scots, 1550-1590; c, German, 1510-1540; d, French, 1550-1558; e, English, 1630-1650; f, French, 1660-1680.

Some of our schools of design exhibit the work of their students on dolls made for the purpose. The Traphagen School of Design of New York City is a noteworthy example. Through their courtesy two of these dolls (121, a and b) are reproduced here. Drawing a is another interpretation of Marie Antoinette, this with an elaborate costume; b is sixteenth century Eleanor of Toledo. The

120. Six Costume Dolls from The Metropolitan Museum of Art, New York, N. Y.

  a: French Costume, 1420–1460.

  b: French Costume in the Style of Mary, Queen of Scots, 1550–1590.

  c: German Costume, 1510–1540.

  d: French Costume, 1550–1558.

  e: English Costume, 1630–1650.

  f: French Costume, 1660–1680.

121. Two Portrait Dolls from The Traphagen School of Design, New York, N. Y.

a: Marie Antoinette, Eighteenth Century.

b: Eleanor of Toledo, Sixteenth Century.

122. Two Dolls Representing Characters in Fiction by Muriel Atkins Bruyere, New York, N. Y.

a: Scarlett O'Hara, from the Novel, "Gone With the Wind," by Margaret Mitchell.

b: Alice in Wonderland, from the Story by Lewis Carroll.

costume was adapted from Bronzino's portrait painting of Eleanora and her son Ferdinando.

Characters from story books are always interesting. Mrs. Muriel Atkins Bruyere of New York City has made a number of fascinating dolls of this character. Through her kindness, two of these are reproduced here. They are Scarlett O'Hara from the famous novel "Gone With the Wind" by Margaret Mitchell, and Lewis Carroll's "Alice in Wonderland."

No. 123 is another Alice, sketched from an old doll. The stockings or socks of the doll were made from a pair of discarded striped socks of a small child.

123. Alice, Sketched from an Old Doll.

124. Walking Costume of 1815. (Ensemble of Mme. Lavelette, in which her husband made his escape from prison.)

The dress is blue with bands of red and white around the skirt to match the red and white stripes of the socks. Collar and apron are plain white batiste, the latter with a ruffle around the edge.

Most interesting of all are the characters from real life stories interpreted by dolls. No. 124, a walking costume of 1815, belonged to Mme. Lavelette, and was the outfit in which her husband made his escape from prison.

People in general are familiar only with portraits of Martha Washington past the prime of life, which is regrettable, for she was handsome in her youth.

No. 125 shows a young Martha, taken from an old engraving. This is a good example of the mid-eighteenth century Watteau costume.

No. 126 shows the hooped skirt of 1740, revived a hundred years later in an exaggerated form.

125. Mid-Eighteenth Century Costume.
(A young Martha Washington.)

126. Hooped Skirt of 1740. (Revived a hundred years later in an exaggerated form.)

No. 127 is a costume of 1793. It would be simple to make in miniature, and very effective in dainty lace or net with an over-dress of china silk or light-weight brocade.

Some of the most artistic costumes of the past come to us through great paintings by old masters. Following the example of Mrs. Bruyere and others who have made charming dolls of "Pinkie" by Lawrence and "The Blue Boy" by Gainsborough, an equally attractive pair could be done of Princess Mary Stuart and William II of Orange from the portrait by Van Dyck. No. 128 is

Above. 128. Seventeenth Century Children's Costumes.

Left. 127. Costume of 1793.

sketched from the painting. Also, the young dauphin who became in theory Louis XVII of France and his sister, Madame Royale, (Marie Therese Charlotte) children of the unfortunate Marie Antoinette, would make interesting dolls to show the costume of young persons at about the close of the eighteenth century. (See Sketch 129.)

Dress between the year 1819 and 1900 could be represented by Victoria dolls. In literature easily obtained at public libraries there are numerous pictures of the great queen from early childhood to old age.

Boy dolls, difficult to dress satisfactorily, could be most pleasing as Pepito Costa Y. Bonello (see Sketch No. 130, after the painting by Goya) in the costume of about 1800; Master Anthony de Rothschild (1892) by Millais (No. 131 is an interpretation) and the fictional character "Little Lord Fauntleroy" by Mrs. Frances Hodgson Burnett (No. 132), published in 1886, the original illustration by Reginald Birch.

Many have attempted to dress the "lady" doll in "period" gown; why not the "child"? The latter would make a refreshing variety. What a gorgeously

ON DRESSING THE "PERIOD" DOLL

129. Children's Costumes of 1793. (After contemporary paintings of the Dauphin and Madame Royale of France.)

130. Boy's Costume of 1800. (After the painting by Goya.)

131. Boy's Costume of 1892. (After a picture by John Everett Millais.)

132. Boy's Costume of 1886. (After the fictional character, "Little Lord Fauntleroy," by Frances Hodgson Burnett.)

costumed "baby" could be made from the child in Frans Hals' "Nurse and Child." Equally attractive would be dolls modeled from the children in the paintings by Reynolds, Lawrence, Velasquez and other famous painters of childhood.

It would be interesting if doll clubs throughout the country would specialize each in different periods of historic dress, one group taking the development of the first woven costume, the tunica, with its changing length and form of skirt and sleeve; other groups, the varying styles of a given century from early times down to the present day. A national exhibition, perhaps sponsored by those who have dolls to sell, when all these creations might be brought together, would make a show that would capture the imagination of everyone. And it might create even greater interest if some of these dolls, historic figures of the past with stories to tell, could be brought to life through the medium of that most ancient of theatres, the marionette stage.

Chapter X

On Making Dolls to Represent America's First Ladies

IT is an ambition of many collectors to have a full set of dolls showing America's First Ladies, not only because they represent examples of period clothes, but because the history of America is associated with such a set. So far these dolls have not been likenesses of the White House hostesses, merely costume exhibitions; it has been difficult to find portraits of the ladies. The manikins showing the dresses of the hostesses of the Executive Mansion in the Smithsonian Institution, Washington, D. C., are not models of the women themselves. The purpose of the accompanying sketches is to enable collectors and doll makers to

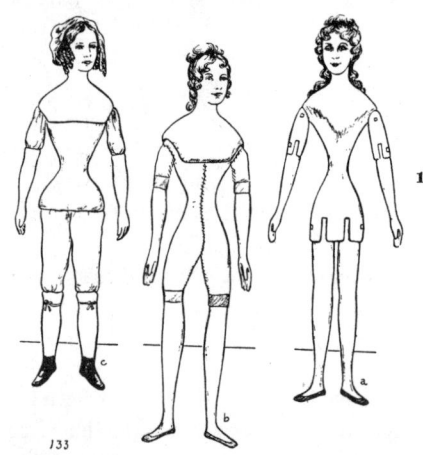

133. **Type of Doll Bodies Popular During the Reign of the Earlier "First Ladies."**

a: A Miniature "Martha Jefferson."

b: A Miniature "Dolly Madison."

c: A Miniature "Sarah C. Polk."

obtain a more accurate idea of what these ladies actually looked like. It has not been possible to find a picture of Betty Taylor Bliss-Dandridge. According to the findings of Miss Margaret W. Brown, curator of history at the Institution, Mrs. Dandridge refused to pose for a portrait.

It is interesting to note the kind of doll bodies popular during the reign of the earlier First Ladies. The accompanying sketches (No. 133) show (a) a wooden peg-jointed doll that might have been used for a miniature Martha Jefferson when the young lady was a schoolgirl of sixteen in 1788; (b) a kid body with wooden arms and legs popular in Dolly Madison's time; (c) a cloth body with china arms and legs that undoubtedly would have been used with a china head representing Sarah C. Polk or any later china-headed representation of a First Lady. If one is planning to use a modeled head in doll making, this latter pattern would be a good one to use. Sketched features on a cloth head can be made attractive. Higgins varicolored inks are helpful in this respect. Just a touch of rouge gently blended with a finger tip is effective when properly applied. If oil paint is used, be sure to select cloth that "takes" kindly to it, one that is not too absorbent. Try samples before deciding on the material to use for the finished product.

Some of the First Ladies undoubtedly had their china representatives, but proofs are not easy to find. A china-headed doll known to collectors as "Dolly Madison" has the ear-marks of a later doll, but an earlier one with somewhat similar hairdo, more oval eyes and a longer neckline might easily have been made to represent so famous a person, for it is of the right period.

A Parian doll made at about the time Mrs. Lincoln presided at the White House, shows a wreath of flowers in the hair—Mary Todd's favorite coiffure—but whether or not this actually represented Mrs. Lincoln is not known. A doll supposed to represent the lady just before she was married, shows her with a bow on either side of the head, the back hair held in a snood. The latter was used for a walking doll of the eighteen sixties, and was called "The Patent Autoperipatetikos Walking Doll." Directions for its operation are given on the lid of the box. It is possible that various models of the china head were used for this "walking doll." The hairdo of the doll pictured on the box lid does not tally with at least one of these "walking" dolls. However, the patent was for the mechanics of the doll, not the head. It is possible, but not probable, that both these heads were made to represent Mary Todd Lincoln.

The only commercial doll that we definitely can connect with a First Lady is recent, a beautiful "lady" manufactured by Mrs. Emma C. Clear of Redondo Beach, California, and is one of a pair—"George and Martha Washington." We know that notables have been represented in doll form over a long period of years, although it is doubtful that many of the First Ladies were prominent enough to be so distinguished. Famous singers and actresses of the past, as well as the present, have been honored in this way. Pauline Stanton in "The Puritan" for November, 1899, lists some of the actresses and favorites of fiction made in doll form—Maude Adams as the Lady Babbie in "The Little Minister;" Julia Arthur as the Lady of Quality; Glory Quayle "in toboggan cap and jersey;" Roxanne of Rostand's "Cyrano de Bergerac;" Ada Rehan as Portia; and the famous singer Adelina Patti. Miss Stanton does not mention Jenny Lind, but we have many evidences that such a doll was made.

It would be interesting if we could know definitely just which, if any, of the White House personages were represented in the dolls of other days. A china swivel-headed doll that looks like an infantile "George Washington" was sold at a Sanitary Fair in Baltimore during the Civil War, but there is no proof of its identity with that illustrious person. The doll was among a collection in a large wooden shoe at the Fair, and it is said that Lincoln showed a keen interest in the exhibit. The present owner is Claire Fawcett, the writer's daughter.

If hairdo were proof of a doll's identity, the task of identification would be simple. Many of the White House ladies wore coiffures that have been reproduced in dolls, but of course any popular hair arrangement would be used by

ON MAKING DOLLS TO REPRESENT AMERICA'S FIRST LADIES   111

manufacturers of dolls. It is interesting to compare the coiffure of such ladies as Angelica Van Buren, Abigail Fillmore, Jane Appleton Pierce, Sarah C. Polk, Harriet Lane, Lucretia Rudolph Garfield, Ida Saxton McKinley and others with those of the china dolls of their respective days. One will find hair styles repeat, for example, an older china doll wears the same hair arrangement as Ida Saxton McKinley, who was hostess in the Executive Mansion from 1897 to 1901.

A brief description of America's First Ladies follows.

MARTHA WASHINGTON, (Mrs. George Washington) (No. 134) 1789-1797.

America's first "Leading Lady" never saw the White House. In 1789 New York was the Capital city; Philadelphia the next seven years.

When the young and handsome Martha Dandridge Custis met Colonel George Washington, she was a wealthy widow after a marriage of eight years to

134. Martha Washington, America's
First Presiding Lady, 1789-1797.

Daniel Parke Custis. Only two of her four children of that marriage were still living. These were little Martha and John or Jack as he was called.

Soon after her second marriage, George and Martha and the two children moved to Mount Vernon on the Potomac, where many thousands of visitors have since thronged to wander about the fine old house and gardens which the Washington family had loved in the long ago, but where George was seldom seen when the duties of his high office, first as commander-in-chief of the armies of his country, and later as President of the new republic, kept him away from the most precious things in a man's life—his home, his wife and his children; in this case, his adopted children.

Lady Washington, as she was called, accompanied the General whenever it was possible, and she saw the evacuation of Boston, but there were seven years when he had to be away from his beloved "Patsy," as he affectionately called his wife.

Martha survived her children and her husband. When the latter passed away she was kneeling at the foot of his bed. " 'Tis well" she said calmly, "all is now over; I shall soon follow him; I have no more trials to pass through." She spoke truly, for within two years, at the age of seventy, she joined her husband in that place in which there is no more parting.

The manikin which represents this celebrated lady in the Smithsonian Institution is seated in one of Martha's own chairs by one of her own tables. In one hand is a brown silk embroidered bag made by the lady herself. Her dress

135. Abigail Smith Adams, Second Presiding Lady, 1797-1801.

is of hand-painted salmon colored silk with wild flower and insect all-over designs, and is trimmed at intervals with green jewel ornaments. The skirt is made of straight widths, gathered with fullness to a basque pointed at front and back.

ABIGAIL SMITH ADAMS, (Mrs. John Adams, No. 135) Second Hostess of America's Executive Mansion, First Hostess of the White House, 1797-1801.

Abigail Adams was the first lady actually to preside at the White House, although she did so for only six months. Before that time, Philadelphia was the Capital city. John Adams was elected President after a long political career during which he and his wife travelled abroad extensively on the business of the new nation. Mrs. Adams was the wife of the second president of the United States and the mother of the sixth. And no woman could have been more worthy of such a distinction. Her letters to her son, and the wise advice she gave him might be imitated profitably by every parent. On one occasion she wrote: "Suffer me to recommend to you one of the most useful lessons of life, the knowledge and study of yourself. There you run the greatest hazard of being deceived. Self-love and partiality cast a mist before the eyes, and there is no knowledge so hard to be acquired, nor of more benefit when once thoroughly understood. . . . learn betimes, from your own observations and experience, to govern and control yourself. Having once obtained this self-government, you will find a foundation laid for happiness to yourself and usefulness to mankind." If everyone

136. Martha Jefferson Randolph, Third Presiding Lady, 1801-1809.

would take this advice seriously, there would be no more wars. A study of the life and letters of Mrs. Adams is an inspiration. She is one of only three wives of American presidents that Mrs. Sarah Jane Hale included in her volume, "Distinguished Women." Martha Washington and Dolly Madison are the other two.

It has not been an easy matter to obtain costumes to represent the earlier wives of the presidents. The great grandsons of Mrs. Adams remarked that their ancestors were not in the habit of keeping their old clothes. But another near relative of the Adams family in Salem, Mass., Miss Susan Osgood, came forward with a plainly made but handsomely embroidered dress of dark greenish blue Canton crepe. The waist is trimmed with plum colored silk and lace. Lemon colored slippers are worn by the Institution manikin, and in the hand is a fan with ivory sticks. Roman pearls complete the ensemble.

MARTHA JEFFERSON RANDOLPH, (Mrs. William Mann Randolph, No. 136) Administration of Thomas Jefferson, 1801-1809.

Martha Jefferson Randolph, the elder of two sisters, had been motherless for nineteen years when her father accepted the duties of President of the United

States. There was no official hostess of the White House during the Jefferson administration, but Martha and on occasion Mrs. Madison acted in this capacity. Martha was used to mingling with persons of distinction, and her education and travels abroad helped to fit her for a high social position.

In response to a request from the family for a costume to represent Mrs. Randolph in the Museum collection, her great grandson, Colonel Jefferson Randolph Kean, wrote that all the old Jefferson dresses had been cut up and worn to rags by the Southern girls during the Civil War. But one of her descendants, Miss Fanny Burke of Alexandria, Va., owned a long, dark blue cloak with paisley-like trimmings belonging to her great grandmother, and this she gladly contributed. The contemporary dress is of embroidered batiste over pale pink silk. Mrs. Randolph's prayer book and handkerchief were also given to the Museum.

The head in the sketch is copied from an engraving made of Martha Jefferson when she was about sixteen years old. At the time she served in the White House, her hairdo was probably similar to the one worn by the Museum manikin—short hair under a turban, the height of fashion about 1800.

After the President's term had expired, father and daughter retired to Monticello, where Martha cared for him until his death two years later, when the house was sold.

DOROTHY PAINE TODD MADISON (Mrs. James Madison, No. 137) 1809-1817.

The love and veneration of a great and good person lives on through the years long after the last sleep has put an end to all earthly ties. So it was with Dorothy Paine Todd Madison. James Madison was admired and respected, but his wife, Dolly, as we know her, was wholeheartedly loved by all who came under her influence. As before stated, she was one of the three wives of American presidents recorded by Mrs. Hale as a truly great person. At a time when there was violent opposition to the government and bitter animosity in opposing parties, hatred was softened in the presence of this fine woman with her generous and kindly spirit and genuine love of people. Dolly Madison cared nothing for formality. Her table was more abundant than elegant. When she received a report that the wife of a foreign minister had remarked that her table was "more like a harvest-home supper than the entertainment of a secretary of state" she answered her informant smilingly that she thought "abundance was preferable to elegance; that circumstances formed customs, and customs formed taste; and as the profusion, so repugnant to foreign customs, arose from the happy circumstance of the superabundance and prosperity of our country, she did not hesitate to sacrifice the delicacy of European taste for the less elegant, but more liberal fashion of Virginia."

Some of the less fortunate children of the District of Columbia are still benefitting by the liberality of Mrs. Madison; she was partly responsible for founding an asylum in 1812 for war orphans which still is operating. It is one of the happiest places of its kind the writer ever has visited.

When, in 1817, the Madisons retired to his paternal estate, Montpelier in Virginia, Mr. Madison's ninety-seven-year-old mother made the remark: "Dolly

**137. Dorothy Paine Madison,
Fourth Presiding Lady, 1809-1817.**

is my mother now, and tenderly cares for all my wants." The erstwhile little Quaker girl has left a name in American history which never will be forgotten.

Dolly Madison's dress in the Smithsonian Institution is of pale yellow satin, the over-skirt embroidered in silver wheat design, the under-skirt with beautiful Chinese embroidery. A plain bodice is trimmed with cream colored Point lace, and a graceful shawl drapes the shoulders.

ELIZABETH KORTRIGHT MONROE, (Mrs. James Monroe, No. 138) 1817-1825.

MARIA HESTER MONROE GOUVERNEUR, (No. 139) 1817-1825.

The etiquette of the White House with Mrs. James Monroe as hostess was in direct contrast to that of her predecessor. Elizabeth Kortright had absorbed formality by attendance at foreign courts, and also was influenced by her daughter, Mrs. George Hay, who had been educated at Madame Campan's, the school of the nobility of France. "Elegance, dignity and charm" were accorded her by the writers of the day. She travelled a great deal, and on one occasion when she visited Paris was able to save the life of Madame de Lafayette, intervening on the very day the unfortunate woman was to have been executed.

Mrs. Monroe's gown (from the Costume Exhibition of the James Monroe Law Office National Shrine in Fredericksburg, Va.) is made of rich cream silk brocade with a colorful design of red and yellow flowers. It is a fine example of the "sacque" period, and shows the Watteau pleated back. Round and oblong "buttons" edged with lace trim the over-skirt.

For some time the only costume representing the Monroe administration in the National Museum was that of Maria Hester Monroe Gouverneur, (No. 139) younger daughter of the President and his wife, and the first White House bride. The costume is so lovely that it has been decided to keep it in the collection. It is light blue in color, the flounces and bodice elaborately trimmed with sheaves

138. Elizabeth Kortright Monroe, (Mrs. James Monroe) Fifth Presiding Lady, 1817-1825.

139. Maria Hester Monroe Gouverneur, (Mrs. Samuel Laurence Gouverneur) younger daughter of President James Monroe.

of golden wheat. Straw braid on the waist is hand made, and the back pleated in Watteau style.

In the glass case which holds this figure in the Museum is a table brought from France by President Monroe, and on it, with pieces of silver, a fan and some music books, is an old-fashioned mirror made from one of the fragments of glass broken by British soldiers in the White House in 1812.

LOUISA CATHERINE JOHNSON ADAMS (Mrs. John Quincy Adams, No. 140) 1825-1829.

John Quincy Adams, then Monroe's secretary of state, met and married Louisa Catherine Johnson in the place of her birth, England. She was the daughter of the American Consul General to London and a French woman.

After John Quincy's father became President of the United States, the younger Adams was transferred to Berlin, and later came with his wife to America. He became minister to Russia for six years, then minister to England, and finally, in 1825, President of the United States. At the time Mrs. Adams was not in good health, but, notwithstanding this, she entertained royally and made a gracious hostess at the White House.

140. Louisa Catherine Adams, (Mrs. John Quincy Adams) Sixth Presiding Lady, 1825-1829.

The Museum costume representing Louisa Catherine is typical of the period—short waist, rather tight skirt with "birthday cake" decorations, puffed sleeves and low neck line. It is of tulle over white silk, and silver braid edges the ruffles. The amazing fact about this frail looking material is its remarkable condition after more than a hundred years of existence. Even the silver braid is untarnished.

EMILY DONELSON, (No. 141, Andrew Jackson's Administration) 1829-1836;

SARAH YORKE JACKSON, (No. 142, Mrs. Andrew Jackson, Jr.) 1831-1837.

During Andrew Jackson's administration, with the exception of the last year, the duties of hostess fell to Emily Donelson, wife of the late Mrs. Jackson's

141. Emily Donelson, (Mrs. Andrew Jackson Donelson) Seventh Presiding Lady, 1829-1836. (She served in lieu of Rachel Donelson Jackson, wife of President Andrew Jackson.)

142. Sarah Yorke Jackson, (Mrs. Andrew Jackson, Jr.) Presiding Lady the last year of the Jackson Administration, 1837, and assistant to Mrs. Donelson 1831-1836.

nephew, later assisted by Sarah Yorke Jackson, who came as a bride to the White House in 1831, and spent her time between the Hermitage, the old Jackson estate in Tennessee, and the Executive Mansion. Emily, though young, was capable. Her parties made the White House a lively place. And her four children born there certainly added to the gaiety.

Mrs. Mary R. Wilcox, granddaughter of Emily Donelson, sent the Museum what was left (after a fire) of the inaugural gown worn by her grandmother, together with a high-backed tortoise-shell comb and numerous relics given by Jackson admires. The dress in the Smithsonian exhibition was a gift of President Jackson himself, for Emily died before Jackson passed on. The basque of tannish cloth is delicately embroidered with tiny pink flowers. Tulle softens the neckline, and is caught up at the front and shoulders with a cluster of flowers. A white lace skirt covers light tan silk.

After the death of Emily in 1836, Sarah Yorke Jackson, Mrs. Andrew Jackson, Jr. became official hostess. She was young, vivacious and attractive. Her husband had been born a Donelson, a nephew of the President's wife, but had been adopted in infancy by Andrew Jackson. Mrs. J. Cleves Symmes of Atlanta, Georgia, granddaughter of Sarah Yorke Jackson, was kind enough to furnish a photograph of her grandmother, from which the head in the sketch was made.

Mrs. Harry Evans, at that time president of the Hermitage Association of Tennessee, presented the Smithsonian with the wedding gown shown in the sketch, and also a picture of Mrs. Jackson. The dress is of embroidered gauze with a plain white satin sleeveless low-necked bodice encircled with a deep collar of Duchesse lace falling gracefully over the shoulders. The manikin in the Smithsonian carries a long lace scarf.

SARAH ANGELICA SINGLETON VAN BUREN, (Mrs. Abraham Van Buren, No. 143) 1839-1841.

Sarah Angelica Singleton Van Buren was the President's daughter-in-law. She had met Major Abraham Van Buren when only a schoolgirl visiting Dolly Madison, and was still very young when, as a bride, she entered the White House to serve as hostess.

Sarah Angelica's gown is of royal blue velvet measuring about nine yards around the hem, and is worn over a hoop skirt. A handsome cream lace barb trims the low-necked dress, and one of the large handkerchiefs so characteristic of the times, is held in one hand. Portraits of the lady, as well as the Museum manikin, show the three-feathered headdress. We are indebted to Mrs. Green of Columbia, S. C., a niece of Mrs. Van Buren, for the outfit.

MRS. WILLIAM HARRISON, JR.; JANE IRWIN FINDLAY, (Mrs. James Findlay, No. 144) Administration of William Henry Harrison, 1841.

William Henry Harrison's sojourn in the White House started with much fanfare, but a month later he was carried out in a coffin. So it was that the

143. Angelica Van Buren, (Mrs. Abraham Van Buren, Eighth Presiding Lady, 1839-1841.

144. Jane Irwin Findlay, (Mrs. James Findlay) Ninth Presiding Lady, (in lieu of Anna Symmes Harrison, wife of President William Henry Harrison) 1841.

services of his young daughter-in-law, the widow of his son, Wm. Henry Harrison, Jr., and her mother by adoption, Jane Irwin Findlay, as White House hostesses, were very brief indeed. Harrison's wife never saw the White House, for the weather had been too stormy for the frail lady to make the journey at the time of her husband's inauguration.

The Museum was not able to obtain a costume belonging to either Mrs. Harrison Senior or Junior, but the costume of Jane Irwin Findlay is a splendid example of the period. The full skirt is made of straight widths attached to a plain bodice relieved with a white collar, and the sleeves are leg-of-mutton style.

Anna Symmes Harrison, the President's wife, deserves a place in our thoughts. She was the devoted mother of ten children, and had the sorrow of seeing one baby, three grown daughters, four sons and ten grand-children die during a period of thirty years at North Bend, Indiana Territory.

LETITIA CHRISTIAN TYLER, (Mrs. John Tyler the First, No. 145) 1841-1842;

JULIA GARDINER TYLER, (Mrs. John Tyler the Second, No. 146) 1844-1845.

Letitia Christian, President Tyler's first wife, lived scarcely two years after her husband's inauguration. Since she was very delicate, the duties of hostess at the White House generally devolved upon Mrs. Robert Tyler, daughter-in law of the President.

Julia Gardiner of Gardiner's Island, N. Y., became the wife of John Tyler in 1844. It was only by a lucky chance the soon to be married couple were not

Left: (145 at top) Letitia C. Tyler (Mrs. John), Tenth Presiding Lady, 1841-42.
(146) Julia G. Tyler, Presiding Lady 1844-45 of the Tenth Administration.

blown to bits when, on a presidential boating party down the Potomac on the Princeton, a gun exploded and killed Miss Gardiner's father and several members of Tyler's cabinet.

It was Mrs. Julia Tyler's daughter, Mrs. Pearl Tyler Ellis, who sent the dress to represent her daughter to the Museum. It is fashioned of mellowed white gauze colorfully embroidered.

SARAH CHILDRESS POLK, (Mrs. James Knox Polk, No. 147) 1845-1849.

Sarah Childress Polk was still in her teens when she married James Knox Polk, then a member of the legislature of Tennessee. The following year, as a congressman, he began a long career in Washington, ending in the Presidency of the United States in 1845.

While Mrs. Polk was a strict Presbyterian, and frowned upon dancing, nevertheless, she was a popular hostess, a noted conversationalist, and devoted her time to White House duties. Having no child of her own, she adopted a daughter.

For a long time the Museum was not able to find a dress to represent her, then one of the members of the Committee read about a fancy dress ball given in New York, at which one of the dancers wore the inaugural ball dress formerly belonging to Sarah Polk. When the owner of the costume was finally traced, she proved to be Mrs. Sarah Polk Fall, the adopted daughter of the former Pres-

147. Sarah Childress Polk, (Mrs. James Knox Polk), Eleventh Presiding Lady, 1845-1849

ident's wife. Mrs. Fall gave the gown to the Museum. It is of blue satin brocaded in an all-over design of the poinsetta flower (named in honor of Joel Poinsett of South Carolina) and is trimmed with blonde lace and ribbon bows.

BETTY TAYLOR BLISS-DANDRIDGE, (Mrs. Philip Dandridge, No. 148) Administration of Zachary Taylor, 1849-1850.

"Miss Betty," as Zachary Taylor's youngest daughter was called even after her marriage to Mr. Dandridge, served as White House hostess in place of Mar-

148. Costume of Betty Taylor Bliss-Dandridge, Twelfth Presiding Lady, 1849-1850. (She served in place of her mother, Margaret Smith Taylor, wife of President Zachary Taylor.)

garet Smith Taylor, the President's wife. Since "Miss Betty" refused to pose for a picture, there is none available, and the sketch is of Margaret in her daughter's costume. This dress, a plaid silk edged with lace at the bodice, was formerly green, but it has faded to a soft brown. Black mitts and a handkerchief embroidered with the name "Betty" accompany the Museum representation of "Miss Betty." She was young and charming and well-liked during her brief reign at the Executive Mansion. Mrs. Taylor had no social ambitions and much preferred her quiet home life in Baton Rouge, La., to the limelight of residence in the White House.

Zachary Taylor died only sixteen months after he became President, and his wife survived him by a brief two years.

149. Abigail Powers Fillmore. (Mrs. Millard Fillmore) Thirteenth Presiding Lady, 1850-1853.

ABIGAIL POWERS FILLMORE (Mrs. Millard Fillmore, No. 149) 1850-1853.

Millard Fillmore owed much of his success in life to Abigail Powers, his teacher before she became his wife. It was Mrs. Fillmore who was responsible for the establishment of the White House library. Her keen sense of humor and fine character shone in her kindly eyes, and although she had known poverty and hardship in early youth, they had softened, rather than hardened her. When her husband became President of the United States, Abigail filled her new position admirably, but owing to increasingly poor health, brought on no doubt by a too strenuous early life, their young daughter Mary Abigail many times relieved her mother as hostess. It was not long after Fillmore's term expired that his wife passed away.

By advertising, the Museum contacted Mrs. Frances Hubbard Larkin of Buffalo, N. Y., who had a costume belonging in the Fillmore family, and although Mrs. Larkin hesitated, for sentimental reasons, to part with the gown (even bringing it to Washington and returning with it three times) she finally gave it to the Museum. The costume is of lavender silk trimmed with a flower figured flounce. The low-necked, short-sleeved basque is pointed front and back and covered with a lace scarf, which falls over the shoulders to the lace trimming of the sleeves. In the hand of the Museum manikin is a handkerchief attached to a ring on the little finger.

It is interesting to note the coiffure shown in the sketch of Mrs. Fillmore. Straight ringlets, chin length, were typical of the eighteen fifties, and there are still extant a surprising number of old dolls with this hair arrangement.

150. Jane Appleton Pierce, (Mrs. Franklin Pierce) Fourteenth Presiding Lady, 1853-1857.

JANE APPLETON PIERCE (Mrs. Franklin Pierce, No. 150) 1853-1857.

Jane Appleton Pierce was a New Englander with the love of home typical of New Englanders. She was not particularly happy about being a "first lady," and the sudden death (in a railroad accident) of her only remaining child, a boy of fourteen, made her very sad. Nevertheless, she attended all functions at the White House which necessitated the presence of a hostess, and carried herself well. Mrs. Pierce had been brought up in an atmosphere of culture. Her father was a minister and also President of Bowdoin College.

The hairdo in the sketch is quite different from the Museum manikin, but it is authentic; in fact, is from a portrait of the lady herself. The dress is of black tulle embroidered in silver dots, and is the one worn by Mrs. Pierce at her husband's inaugural ball.

HARRIET LANE JOHNSTON, No. 151 (Administration of James Buchanan;) 1857-1861.

Harriet Lane was "to the Manor born" and particularly fitted to become America's leading lady. She was brought up by her uncle, James Buchanan, after being left an orphan at nine years of age. Part of her education was gained through travel abroad. "Uncle James" was appointed Minister to England in 1852, and blonde, attractive young Harriet accompanied him. The twenty-year-old girl was quite a favorite in court circles.

On Making Dolls to Represent America's First Ladies 125

151. Harriet Lane Johnston, (Mrs. Henry
Eliot Johnston) Fifteenth Presiding Lady,
(James Buchanan's Administration)
1857-1861.

Three years after Buchanan became President of the United States, and while Miss Lane was hostess at the White House, the late King Edward VII, who was Prince of Wales at the time, visited America and was entertained at the Executive Mansion. Later, when the Prince became King, Harriet was especially invited to the coronation ceremony.

The portrait sketch shows the lady in her wedding gown. It is of white moire antique silk, and the very wide skirt is prettily tabbed around the bottom. The Smithsonian manikin shows the point lace bridal veil worn as a shawl, and white satin shoes, flat-soled of course, for this was a period when heels were not fashionable.

MARY TODD LINCOLN, (Mrs. Abraham Lincoln, No. 152) 1861-1865.

Mrs. Lincoln shines in the reflected glory of her illustrious husband, one of the greatest men, and surely one of the most loved, in American history. Although Mary Todd was highly respected in her community as a member of one of its most socially prominent families, this alone is far from being enough to make a person live in the hearts of a people. Immediately after her death historians eulogized her, but writers of the present day have gone to the opposite extreme. It might be that she was more ambitious than kind, but it is quite possible that Lincoln needed something that she was able to give. And it must be remembered that it was he who chose her to be his wife. Mary was a woman of sorrows; she had not recovered from the death of her second son when called upon to face the shock of her husband's assassination, and not long after that, the death of her youngest boy. Her mind became unsettled, and although she survived her husband seventeen years, she was not well, and finally died of paralysis in her sister's home at Springfield, Illinois, in 1882.

The Museum manikin representing Mrs. Lincoln wears a costume of royal purple velvet, and carries in one hand a small sunshade, in the other, a fan.

152. Mary Todd Lincoln, (Mrs. Abraham Lincoln) Sixteenth Presiding Lady, 1861-1865.

153. Martha Johnson Patterson, (Mrs. David T. Patterson) Seventeenth Presiding Lady, (Andrew Johnson's Administration) 1865-1869.

Panels in the wide skirt and in the bodice are piped with white silk. The waist is low-necked and short-sleeved, pointed front and back, and trimmed with lace. A relative of the Lincoln family sold this handsome gown to Mrs. Julian-James, who generously gave it to the Museum.

ELIZA MCCARDLE JOHNSON, (Mrs. Andrew Johnson) 1865-1869.

MRS. DAVID T. JOHNSON PATTERSON, (No. 153) active hostess.

It was no easy matter to substitute for so great a person as Abraham Lincoln. This was the position in which Andrew Johnson found himself when he stepped into the place made vacant by the murder of Lincoln. He had a fine helpmate in Eliza McCardel Johnson. She had been his teacher before they were married (when he was but eighteen years of age) and a helpful adviser until the day of his death. Eliza had been through much suffering during the war and this left her an invalid when called to the White House. For this reason their eldest daughter, Mrs. David T. Patterson, took her mother's place as White House hostess, and did so well that all were sorry to see her leave. As a matter of fact, the whole family were very much liked.

The Smithsonian is indebted to Mrs. Patterson's son for the white camel's hair evening wrap which had formerly belonged to his mother. The gown is of flowered brocade.

On Making Dolls to Represent America's First Ladies

154. Julia Dent Grant, (Mrs. Ulysses Simpson Grant) Eighteenth Presiding Lady, 1869-1877.

155. Lucy Ware Webb Hayes, (Mrs. Rutherford B. Hayes) Nineteenth Presiding Lady, 1877-1881.

JULIA DENT GRANT, (Mrs. Ulysses Simpson Grant, No. 154) 1869-1877.

Many a patriotic American has paused to reflect before the imposing mausoleum on Riverside Drive, New York, known as Grant's Tomb. Few realize how appropriate it is for Mrs. Grant to share the honor of such a monument with her husband. It does not always happen that a faithful wife, after sharing her husband's misfortunes for many years, is rewarded at last by his great victories and triumphs. Such was the case with Mrs. Grant. When the General's two terms as President of the United States expired, Mr. and Mrs. Grant toured the world. Everywhere they went, Grant was hailed as a conquering hero. The wife of China's viceroy gave them a dinner, the first of its kind. And the Emperor of China presented Mrs. Grant with the beautiful white and silver brocade dress which represents the lady in the Museum. The point-lace cape accompanying the manikin was worn at Grant's first inaugural ball. As one may judge from the sketch, taken from a portrait, Mrs. Grant was not a particularly beautiful woman, but she was a devoted wife and mother.

LUCY WARE WEBB HAYES, (Mrs. Rutherford B. Hayes, No. 155) 1877-1881.

Sincerity, good nature and a pleasing personality were qualities which won for Lucy Ware Webb Hayes great popularity at the Executive Mansion. She displeased some by banishing wine from the table, but gained support from temperance advocates. Mrs. Hayes came to the White House well loved by the

Union soldiers under the command of her husband. From the latter she never was long separated, following him about from camp to camp.

A son, Colonel Webb Hayes, sent to the Smithsonian a dress he thought at the time particularly appropriate, for his mother had worn it when she posed for a picture by Daniel C. Huntington. Later he substituted another much handsomer gown, one Mrs. Hayes had worn at a state dinner in honor of the Grand Duke Alexis of Russia when his royal highness visited Washington. It

156. **Lucretia Rudolph Garfield, (Mrs. James A. Garfield) Twentieth Presiding Lady, 1881.**

is of gold brocade trimmed with cream-colored satin, elaborate with beaded bands, fringe, rosettes, panniers, lace and a tabbed skirt with a beautiful train of silk with rosebud pattern. (This was a period of extravagance in dress.) Sleeves are a little below the elbow. Although fancy coiffures were all the rage at this time, Lucy preferred to dress her hair plainly. She was the first college graduate to become the wife of a President of the United States.

LUCRETIA RUDOLPH GARFIELD, (Mrs. James A. Garfield, No. 156) 1881.

Lucretia Rudolph Garfield's stay at the White House was cut short by the assassination of her husband, an event made infinitely more sad by the pain President Garfield suffered for weeks before his death. Mrs. Garfield was a fine woman, well liked, and sympathy in her sorrow was such that a fund of over $350,000 was raised by the public to take care of the family after the tragedy.

Mrs. Garfield was still living when the costume exhibition was started in the Smithsonian, but it was not until a few days before her death that she finally consented to send one of her dresses. It is a good example of the period, when the high neck, long sleeve, pleats, overskirt, bows and rosettes were fashionable. The gown is of lavender satin with a triangular opening at the front. It was worn at the Garfield inaugural ball.

157. Mary Arthur McElroy, (Mrs. John E. McElroy, Chester A. Arthur's Administration) Twenty-first Presiding Lady, 1881-1885.

MARY ARTHUR MCELROY, (Mrs. John E. McElroy, No. 157) Administration of Chester Alan Arthur, 1881-1885.

Mary Arthur McElroy (Mrs. John E. McElroy) was the sister of President Arthur. Owing to the death of her brother's wife, it was she who presided at the White House during Arthur's administration. Mrs. McElroy was a fine-looking woman, simple in her tastes in dress at a time when clothes and hair arrangement were ultra ornate. The President's only child, a girl, was fortunate to be mothered by "Aunt Mary."

Mrs. McElroy's daughters considered the costumes that had formerly belonged to their mother unsuitable to make a good representation of the period, so they had one made—a lovely dress of silver-gray brocade. Black and white cording edges the cuffs and the front panel of the skirt. Beads on cuffs and

158. Frances Folsom Cleveland, (Mrs. Grover Cleveland) Twenty-second Presiding Lady, 1886-1889; 1893-1897.
a: Souvenir Distributed When Baby Ruth Cleveland was born at the White House.

skirt are also black and white. In the lower panel black beads are woven with the design. The bodice is trimmed with lace edging and insertion, the latter intersperced with beads.

FRANCES FOLSOM CLEVELAND, (Mrs. Grover Cleveland, No. 158) 1886-1889; 1893-1897.

Grover Cleveland, second bachelor President to enter the White House, brought his sister, Rose Elizabeth Cleveland, to preside as leading lady. However, the following year he married his ward, Frances Folsom, daughter of his late law partner. Cleveland's romance with this young, vivacious, charming girl excited almost as much interest in America as that of Princess Elizabeth of England's recent romance in our time. And when her first daughter was born in the White House it was an occasion for nation-wide rejoicing. Children were given a tiny commemorative doll fastened on a spray of artificial leaves with a ribbon attached bearing the name "Baby Ruth." (See 158-a).

Mrs. Cleveland's Museum dress was rather disappointing to the Costume Committee, as it is of heavy brocade rather than the light weight material usually worn by the young at that time. It has an all over pattern of roses on a pale green background, full skirt, low neck and short sleeves with girdle and trimming of rose velvet. At the center top of the neck-line is a spread-open butterfly, and a smaller one on the left shoulder. Frances Folsom was the first lady to be married to a President in the White House. She and Mrs. Madison were the youngest wives of Presidents.

159. Caroline Scott Harrison, (Mrs. Benjamin Harrison) Twenty-third Presiding Lady, 1889-1892.

160. Mary Harrison McKee, (Mrs. James Robert McKee) Presiding Lady on the death of her Mother, Mrs. Benjamin Harrison, 1892-1893.

CAROLINE SCOTT HARRISON, (Mrs. Benjamin Harrison, No. 159) 1889-1892;

MARY HARRISON MCKEE, (Mrs. James Robert McKee, No. 160) 1892-1893.

Caroline Scott and Benjamin Harrison (Grandson of William Henry Harrison) were college mates, and Benjamin was still a minor when he and Caroline were married. They celebrated their fortieth anniversary in the White House. She was talented in music and painting, and inherited the literary tastes of her father, president of Oxford College, Ohio. And Benjamin, in his way, was not less talented; he had already attained a seat in the United States Senate when elected to the presidency.

As First Lady, Mrs. Harrison had the help of her daughter Mary (Mrs. James Robert McKee) and when the former died in 1892, Mary assumed all the responsibilities of hostess. Mrs. McKee missed her mother sorely, but she had the comfort of children. Many parties were given for them in the old East Room of the White House. Mrs. McKee was fine looking, and her cordial manners won many friends.

The dress representing Mrs. Caroline S. Harrison is a handsome brocaded affair, the skirt of light plum color over a petticoat of a deeper shade of satin, the bodice light gray; the whole trimmed with purple and gold beads. A handsome sweeping train is draped from the waist-line and ends in a square effect.

161. Ida Saxton McKinley, (Mrs. William McKinley) Twenty-fourth Presiding Lady, 1897-1901.

Mary Harrison McKee's costume shows the typical ornate style of the period. It is of oyster-white brocade trimmed with old gold and dark green velvet, beaded fancy work ending in tassels and a yoke of woven gold beads. Gold-colored shoes, handkerchief, gloves and fan complete the ensemble of the Museum manikin.

IDA SAXTON MCKINLEY, (Mrs. William McKinley, No. 161) 1897-1901.

The McKinley administration was shadowed with tragedy which ended in the assassination of President William McKinley. War with Spain had made the situation grave, and festivities at the White House were temporarily suppressed. Mrs. McKinley was a chronic invalid, and on the night of the inaugural ball she collapsed. Sorrow resulting from the death of their two children was climaxed when in 1901 her husband was assassinated. Mrs. McKinley never recovered from this last great shock.

The ornate Museum dress is the one Mrs. McKinley wore at her husband's inaugural ball, and it still shows the stain made on it when she fell. A large front panel is decorated with pearls in a set design and ends in "tabs." The waist has a high neck, long sleeves and wide revers. Pearl trimming is carried into a high collar. The costume is of heavy cream-colored satin trimmed with Point lace, and the skirt ends in a long train. A lace handkerchief, a gauze and pearl fan, and a bouquet of pink carnations (the McKinley flower) accompany the Smithsonian manikin.

162. **Edith Kermit Carow Roosevelt, (Mrs. Theodore Roosevelt) Twenty-fifth Presiding Lady, 1901-1909.**

EDITH CAROW ROOSEVELT, (Mrs. Theodore Roosevelt, No. 162) 1901-1909.

Edith Carow Roosevelt will be remembered as the wife of one of the most colorful persons in our Presidential history—"Teddy" Roosevelt. Every small boy of the period knew the history of his exploits, and a large set of "hunter" dolls and toy animals with jungle background representing the Roosevelt hunting expeditions to "darkest Africa" was a proud possession of many a lucky American boy. Mrs. William Garrison of Washington, D. C., has a fine example of this set. Other collectors highly prize their "Teddy Roosevelt" doll.

The Smithsonian is indebted to Mrs. Roosevelt's daughter, Mrs. Richard Derby, for the beautiful inaugural dress which adorns the Museum figure made to represent her mother. It is light blue, brocaded with feather swirls in silver and ends in a train, and there is a wide ruffle of Point lace around the low-cut neck-line. In the hands of the Museum manikin is a book telling of Theodore Roosevelt's adventures abroad.

HELEN HERRON TAFT, (Mrs. William H. Taft, No. 163) 1909-1913.

It was like going home to Helen Herron Taft when she became hostess of the White House, for, as a girl of seventeen, when Rutherford Hayes was President, she had visited "Aunt Lucy," as she called Mrs. Hayes. The Herrons and the Hayes were lifelong friends. Mrs. Taft's easy, gracious manner, and her many receptions and garden parties made her a popular hostess. She loved music and established band concerts on the "Speedway."

Helen Herron Taft has the distinction of being the first wife of a President to donate a gown for the exhibition at the Smithsonian. She was still in the

163. Helen Herron Taft, (Mrs. William H. Taft) Twenty-sixth Presiding Lady, 1909-1913.

White House when the Costume Committee was started, and cooperated by giving her inaugural ball dress. It is of white chiffon, Empire style, with a train, and is beautifully embroidered.

ELLEN AXSON WILSON, (Mrs. Woodrow Wilson the First, No. 164) MARGARET WILSON; 1913-1917;

EDITH BOLLING GALT WILSON, (Mrs. Woodrow Wilson the Second, No. 165) 1917-1921.

The first Mrs. Woodrow Wilson (Ellen Axson) endeared herself to all during her brief reign as First Lady of the land, a year and five months. Her dress in the Smithsonian is an example of the hobble skirt period, one of the worst styles in the history of costume. However, it is less objectionable than might be expected; the drapery of the skirt and the train help in this respect. It is of chenille brocade over a lace skirt, trimmed at the sleeves and waist with strings of pearls. Rhinestones help brighten the costume. After her mother's death, August 6, 1914, Margaret assumed the duties of hostess.

The three Wilson girls, Margaret, Jessie and Eleanor, were delighted when their father married again, for they felt that he needed a helpmate, and that Mrs. Galt (Edith Bolling) would prove just that. Her Museum gown is of black velvet with black tulle sleeves. There are jet trimmings on either side of the small train, the latter draped from the waistline. Strings of black beads hang from the low-cut corsage.

The Costume Committee of the Smithsonian Institution had difficulty in obtaining an exhibition dress from the second Mrs. Wilson, as the latter was giving all her time to the President, an invalid during the latter part of his administration. It was a real triumph when this lovely trousseau costume finally came.

164. Ellen Axson Wilson, (Mrs. Woodrow Wilson)
Twenty-seventh Presiding Lady, 1913-1917.

165. Edith Bolling Wilson, (Mrs. Woodrow Wilson)
Twenty-eighth Presiding Lady, 1917-1921.

166. Florence Kling Harding, (Mrs. Warren G. Harding) Twenty-ninth Presiding Lady, 1921-1923.

167. Grace Goodhue Coolidge, (Mrs. Calvin Coolidge) Thirtieth Presiding Lady, 1923-1929.

FLORENCE KLING HARDING, (Mrs. Warren G. Harding, No. 166) 1921-1923.

Tragedy followed the Hardings to the White House, for Warren G. Harding died in 1923, two years before his term was up. Mrs. Harding was preparing to move back to her home in Ohio when approached by a member of the Costume Committee for a dress to add to the collection. She graciously complied. Costumes at that time still showed the influence of the hobble skirt, but this is an example of the best of its kind. The material is white satin with touches of black net with the usual rhinestones and pearl trimmings of the time. Later a handsome opera cloak of blue gauze, trimmed with gilt and blue ostrich feathers, was added to the ensemble.

GRACE GOODHUE COOLIDGE, (Mrs. Calvin Coolidge, No. 167) 1923-1929.

Mrs. Coolidge is a modest, retiring person, respected and liked by the American people. Her gown in the exhibition is the second sent for this purpose, the first one considered by the public not colorful enough to do the lady justice. The accepted one is of American Beauty chiffon velvet, and the short skirt is in three tiers, pointed in front. It is sleeveless, with a low V neck, and a long train hangs from the shoulders. Slippers with rhinestone buckles match the dress. This was the period of short skirts for evening as well as for daytime wear. It looks rather odd in the midst of the other exhibition costumes, which are long.

168. Lou Henry Hoover, (Mrs. Herbert Clark Hoover) Thirty-first Presiding Lady, 1929-1933.

Lou Henry Hoover, (Mrs. Herbert Clark Hoover, No. 168) 1929-1933.

Miss Lou Henry met Herbert Hoover when both were students at Stanford University. They waited to be married only long enough for Lou to be graduated. The young people were devoted to each other, and this devotion lasted throughout the years of their married life; it was a great tragedy for Mr. Hoover when his fine wife died January 7, 1944.

Mrs. Hoover's dress in the Smithsonian, of blue satin, is as unpretentious as the lady herself was. The blouse is draped from the shoulders, the gathers held in place by buckles. It has a low neck and short sleeves. Around the waist is a narrow band of ribbon tied in a double bow at the right. An overskirt on each side ends in a point, and a long, sweeping train is very graceful.

Anna Eleanor Roosevelt, (Mrs. Franklin Delano Roosevelt, No. 169) 1933-1945.

Mrs. Franklin Delano Roosevelt has certainly had more publicity than any other wife of an American President. She has many friends, and her severest critics would have to admit that she is a "do-er" with much to her credit. Her interest in political and educational affairs is well known. She was Vice-Principal of the Todhunter School, New York, and from 1924 to 1928, finance chairman of the Women's Division of the New York State Democratic Committee, and in 1928 a member of the advisory committee in charge of women's activities

169. Anna Eleanor Roosevelt, (Mrs. Franklin Delano Roosevelt) Thirty-second Presiding Lady, 1933-1945.

of the Democratic National Committee. The New York State League of Women voters claims her as a member. While some of her activities ended with her husband's death after twelve years in the White House, she still is intensely interested in politics, and continues to write a daily newspaper column and contribute to magazines. There has hardly been a president's wife active in so many fields or so widely travelled.

The first gown (of blue lace) sent to represent Mrs. Roosevelt has been replaced by a handsome pale pink satin with an ample train. It is simply trimmed at the neckline with a design in pearl beads.

Our present First Lady has quite a different background, although she has always taken a real interest in her husband's political career. During his terms in the Senate she was a valuable aid as his secretary. Despite the demands of Washington's social life, this valiant lady undertook to market and cook for her family until added duties as hostess of the White House made this impossible. She has been active in war work as a member of a cultural and educational organization, the Missouri Chapter of the PEO, but most of her married life has been dedicated to her home, her husband and her daughter. Now whenever possible she takes pleasure in visiting the old tree-shaded rambling house in Independence, Missouri, built by her grandfather Gates in 1864 and which in childhood and early youth she called home.

A dress given by Mrs. Harry S. Truman (nee Bess Wallace) undoubtedly will be added to the Smithsonian collection.

Chapter XI

SHOES

BEFORE dressing a period doll, a study of shoes of the era is advisable. In judging costume, one often looks first at footwear. So it was in the earliest times. The type of shoes worn bespoke the rank of the wearer. At present, they may not denote rank, but they certainly tell something of the character of the wearer.

Like other articles of clothing, shoes first were made for utilitarian purposes. The foot of the Egyptian had to be protected from hot pavements. A simple sandal, a woven straw sole, held over the instep by a thong, served the purpose. In Mesopotamia, where the rainfall was greater, more protection was needed, so heel covering was added, and a thong tied around the big toe held the sandal more securely. A frequent stubbing of toes caused the invention of the turned-up sandal. The Chinese wore wooden-soled moccasins, and those in regions where the cold was acute, shoes of fur. For muddy weather, the Chinese evolved a moccasin with a thick sole of wood, tapering at the bottom and easily lifted from the mud. The Japanese solved the rain and mud problem by wooden pegs fastened to the bottom of the sandal.

In the evolution of the shoe (No. 170), vanity also played a large part. and royal foot deformities sometimes shaped the destiny of the shoe of a given period. Henry VII, who suffered with gout, created a fashion for wide-toed sandals, the width increasing under Henry VIII, and Timur the Lame (Tamerlane) is credited with the introduction of heels (1362) because of a "dropped foot" condition, which made it difficult for him to put his foot to the floor.

In early times (753-27 B. C.), the Greeks considered it quite good form to go barefooted indoors, but not so the Romans. The latter followed the Etruscan method of foot covering rather than the Greek. Slippers called "udo," something like our modern bedroom slippers, were worn in Roman houses, and a similar shoe, but reaching higher up the leg was used for outdoor wear, especially by the peasantry.

The most important footwear of the Romans was the calcei, a leather boot fastened by straps attached at the back part of the uppers. Another important shoe was the "crepida," which left the toes free. Official boots were of red leather. These were worn by senators and high magistrats. Ladies used the same shaped boot, but in various colors, including white. Straps were narrow bands of colored silk.

Early Greeks, No. 172 (600-146 B. C.), boasted a variety of footwear for all classes, the only difference being in the quality and decoration. After 480 B. C. the sandal was universal, and it might have a leather, wood or matting sole. Sometimes these soles were built up to give height to the wearer.

Hunters and horsemen wore high leather boots.

While it was not at all unusual for Greeks of wealth to go barefoot in the house, footwear was an important article of dress. As early as this, shoes were named after distinguished persons.

The transition from sandal to shoe began in the fifth century A. D. in Rome and Constantinople. Leather perforated shoes or sandals fastened on the outside of the ankles were worn a great deal.

The udo before referred to was used at this time, the uppers made of soft leather lined with contrasting silk, the sole of leather. A lady of high rank wore red, the middle classes a dull leather, and the poor untanned hide.

The sixth century was distinguished by beautiful footwear, No. 173, often highly ornamented with jewels set in circles of pearls.

During the seventh, eighth and ninth centuries, footgear did not change much, but the rich wore even more highly ornamented shoes.

In the late thirteenth and early fourteenth centuries, shoes became grotesquely long. No. 170, fig. 5, shows a sandal of the period. They were looped up to the ankle, later to the knee, and finally were attached to the belt. A law then was enacted to restrict the length of the shoe. Only a nobleman might wear his shoes longer than two inches beyond his big toe, and even he was restricted in the matter to not more than two feet beyond his toes!

In England, as the writer has pointed out, shoes became broader under Henry VII, and still broader under Henry VIII. As in the case of the pointed toe, the opposite style was carried to such an extreme that excessive width was prohibited.

During the nineteenth century much was written on the subject of shoes. In "The Delineator, Fashions for March, 1875," we find an interesting article under the heading "Miscellany of Fashion." It reads:

"Our Boots and Slippers.

"We are promised a fresh fashion in our foot coverings, and already there are decided indications of its fulfilment.

"French bonnets suit our tastes almost exactly, but French heels are not acceptable to our reasoning faculties, nor do they agree with our physical organizations. English styles of boots are the kind most liked by sensible women. The wide, low, flat heel, broad sole, and easy natural shape, with a good steel shank to keep them in shape after a walk in the rain, are the qualities that prevail with such ladies as take outdoor exercise. The comfortable boot in which the foot may remain longest without weariness has a double sole, thus hindering a tender foot from bending painfully to every roughness that it touches. This method of construction is not novel, but the materials that are being selected for our Spring wear are quite unlike those of past seasons. For shoes to be worn for evenings or full dress, there are many ladies who furnish their boot makers with pieces of their costumes; but these cannot be worn on the promenade. Now we are assured that prunellas, Farmer satins, or something that is called Francetta cloth, all of which match the colors that are intended for the street, will be used for walking-boots. The boot is foxed with French kid, morocco, or any of the favorite leathers, and is usually in black. We saw a few Russia leather foxings upon boots that were intended for a super-elegant lady of fashion,

SHOES

EVOLUTION OF THE SHOE

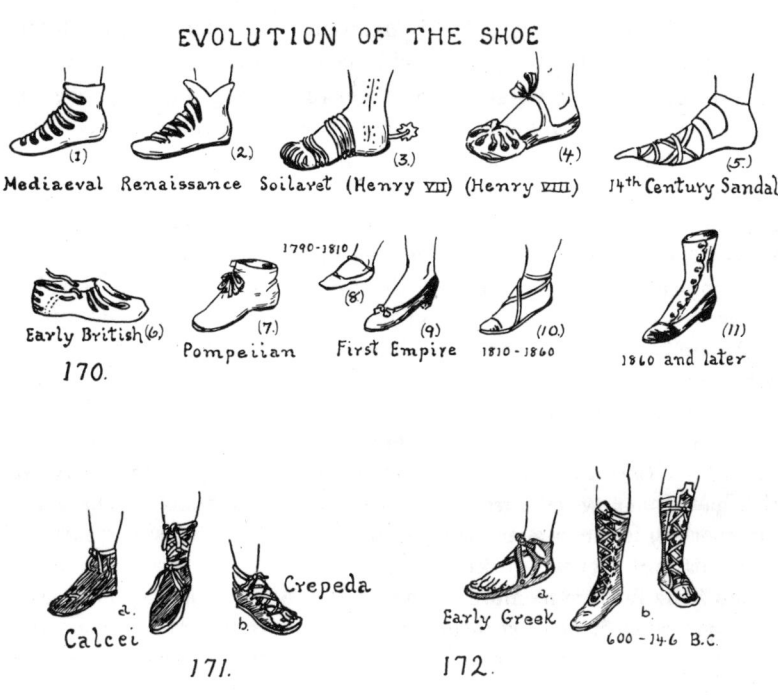

A study of sketches 170 to 173 will give one an idea of where modern shoe designers find inspiration.

and really they were no handsomer than many other sorts of dressed skins, but the cost was something of which my lady was very proud. The only advantage which Russia leathers can have, lies in the grades of color in which they are finished. Even with this advantage, a shapely and graceful outline to the upper edge of a black leather foxing, adds comeliness to the ugliest of feet, and black is harmonious with any color of prunella that may be selected to match the dress.

"For evening wear, white satin boots or slippers are less popular than formerly, partly because they are not serviceable and cannot be renovated, and partly because if there is a defect in a joint of the foot, satin shows it with an aggravating prominence. White kid is handsomer in quality, looks better on the foot, and can be freshened at the glove cleaner's at a trifling expense.

"Flowers are worn upon the toes of evening shoes, but they are in bad taste. A knot of ribbon or a silk bow, with a pearl, burnished steel, or a gilt buckle, is the handsomest decoration for the boot or slipper.

"Children's shoes still exhibit a lavishness in expense, and a vulgarity in their selection, which are exceedingly offensive. Light blue, pink, pale écru, and various other fancy colored kids are seen upon girls in the street, and their lack of appropriateness in the dust of the highway always suggests a hoyden who has escaped from home in an improper plight, or a poor little creature, who, having used up her walking shoes, is obliged to come out in her party boots. The short dress of the young girl always shows her stockings, consequently her boot does not come in contact or direct contrast with the color of her costume, and hence, a black boot or shoe is not only in good taste, but it is positively more attractive. It is a curious fact that the half-grown girl almost always has feet which have somehow managed to get their size in advance of her maturity. This disproportion is much more likely to be observed when she is wearing light boots than with black ones. Black always reduces the apparent size of every thing, which little fact we mention in the interest of such ladies as are ashamed of a No. 5 boot, when it may be a full proof that their feet are in exact proportion to their sizes. In perfect proportion only live the outlines of beauty and harmony."

While the use of the sandal waned for many centuries, it has never completely died out. Today the sandal is almost as popular as it was in mediaeval times. Illustrations 174 and 175 show some of the early sandals, and footwear of the eighteenth and nineteenth centuries. It is probably true that heels (first introduced in 1362) disappeared almost completely with the advent in 1790 of the imitation Greek costume in Europe, but according to an illustration accompanying "The Aesthetics of Dress" by Mrs. Haweis in "The Art Journal" for 1880, a First Empire shoe had small heels. With regard to heeled shoes, Mrs. Haweis says, in the same article: "The re-introduction of heels is barely twenty years old, up to which time various small changes were rung on the Imitation Greek theme, 170, fig. 8, though the theme was thereby obliterated. But the crass and hopeless ugliness, and neglect of all the motifs of grace into which the really well-meant and artistic revival had fallen between 1810 and 1860, like the painful and confused jar which sometimes follows a beautiful carillon, were the most curious tribute to the strength of that terrible reaction which closed the eighteenth century. People all pretended to have something better in their minds than their unworthy looks, and if they had, their looks certainly justified them. But with reviving interest in Art matters came in the heel; not that the heel is artistic, but woman knows it has many merits nevertheless. The origin of heels was probably the advantage of height and protection from mud; but one of the reasons for their recurring popularity is that the foot, like the hand, looks prettier in the tiptoe than the flat position, and for that object a support is needful. So the heel denoted a renewed interest in our 'looks.'"

We wonder how anyone could have worn some of the curious shoes of

SHOES

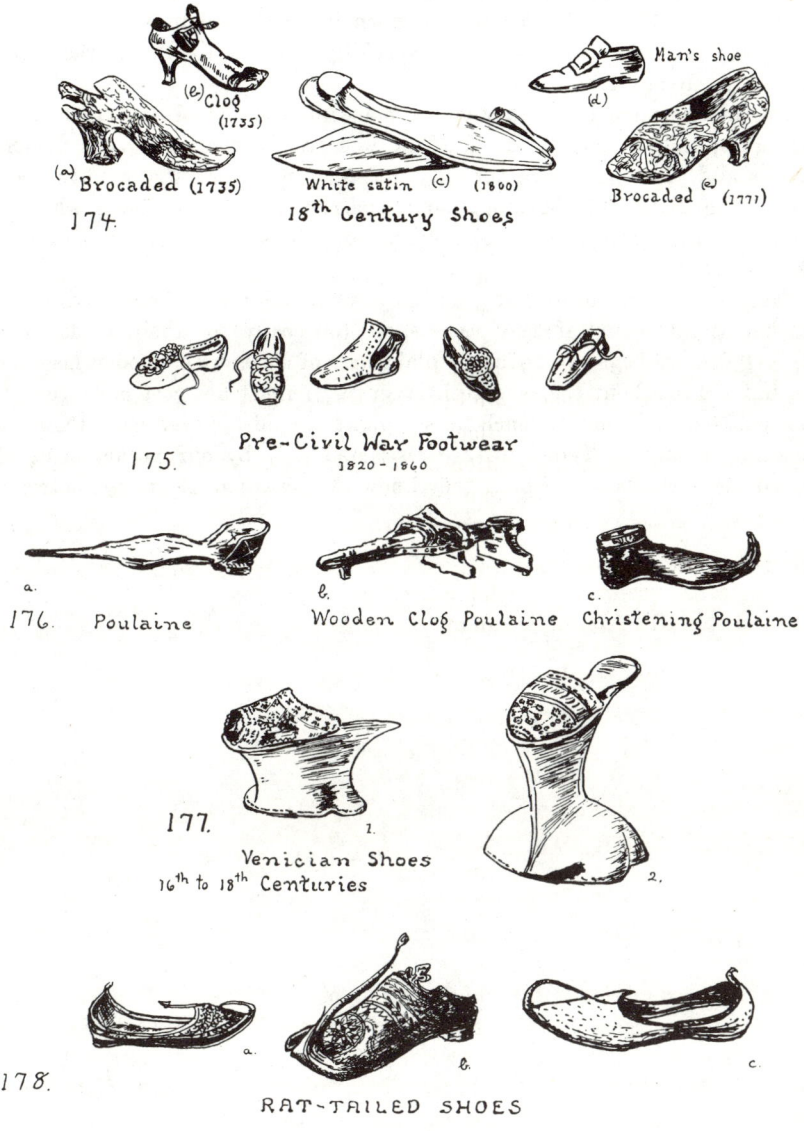

174. 18th Century Shoes — (a) Brocaded (1735); (e) Clog (1735); (c) White satin (1800); (d) Man's shoe; (e) Brocaded (1777)

175. Pre-Civil War Footwear 1820–1860

176. a. Poulaine b. Wooden Clog Poulaine c. Christening Poulaine

177. Venician Shoes 16th to 18th Centuries

178. RAT-TAILED SHOES

In Nos. 174 to 178 above are shown shoes of the Eighteenth Century; Pre-Civil War Footwear; Poulaines; Venician Shoes; and Rat-Tailed Shoes.

other days. No. 176 (a-c) gives an idea of what the poulaines (Polish) or crakowes (English) looked like. The fashion began about 1364, was at its height in 1380 and finally disappeared in 1840. Figure c is a christening poulaine.

No. 177 (1-2) pictures shoes invented to make women stay at home. Some were as high as 18 inches. They were worn in Venice about 1570.

Rat-tailed shoes, No. 178, were especially favored by the Turks. Higher classes wore silver "rat-tails."

For a long time in the history of mankind shoes, fully as much as other wearing apparel, denoted the rank of the wearer. In ancient Greece, models for peasants and patricians were not only different in form, but the color, too, differed. Tragedians wore buskin, Spartan patricians red, courtesans white. The same was true in Rome. Here comedians wore the soccus, from which our word sock is derived.

Even in America in the early days, footwear was rigidly regulated. Citizens were hailed into court if they wore shoes too costly for their station in life. Price regulations began in 1676. A plain pair of shoes with wooden heels (these were worn throughout the seventeenth century) must not cost more than "five pence half penny," but "French falls" might be sold for even more than "seven pence half penny." Today we are restricted only by our pocketbooks. How shocked the ancients would be if they knew the cost of present-day footwear!

Chapter XII

Some Rare Old Dolls

"SEEK and ye shall find"—the saying is just as true today as in Biblical times, when it first was set down. Friends ask the writer: "How do you locate these lovely old dolls?" The answer is plain—by constantly searching. Since the publication of "Dolls—A Guide for Collectors" new examples have turned up, and these new ones are included in this chapter.

No. 179, Miss Bridgewater (a) and Miss Beacon (b), are two of the rarer variety of papiér mâché-headed dolls with kid body and long spindley wooden

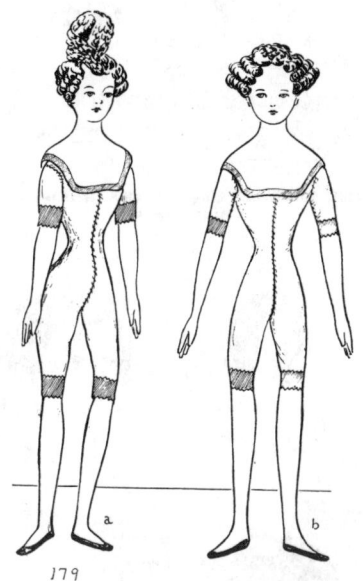

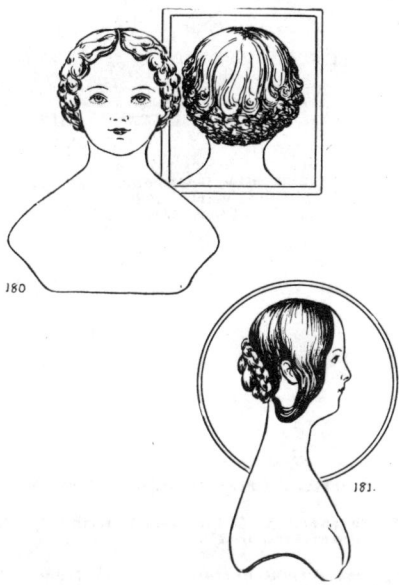

179. (a) Miss Bridgewater. (b) Miss Beacon; both are Antique Papier-mache-headed dolls.

180. Celicia, Brown-eyed China Head with Lower Lashes. 181. Victoria, a Papier-mache Head of the 1820's.

arms and legs. They speak of the time when women wore their hair in an alarming fashion, circa 1828-1833.

Celicia (180) has reason for that contented expression of hers. She is a one-in-a-hundred brown-eyed china beauty with the added distinction of lashes on the lower rather than the upper lid.

No. 181 is Victoria, handed down in a family since the eighteen twenties. Queen Victoria wore her hair in this manner in 1840, although the style was not new at that time. This one is of papiér mâché, but is also found in china.

Few relatives of Miss Goodyear (No. 182) remain for collectors to prize

Her much-braided coiffure makes her especially desirable. She is a fine example of the Goodyear hard rubber doll of 1851, and one of the first to be manufactured from the (then) recently invented substance.

Lavinia, No. 183, is one of the rarest of the china-headed dolls. Curls at the back are caught up with a ribbon band terminating at either end with a flower.

182. Miss Goodyear, a Fine Early Hard Rubber Doll.

183. Lavinia, One of the Rarest of China Heads.

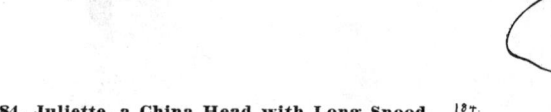

184. Juliette, a China Head with Long Snood.
185. Heather, A China Head with Feather Decorations in Hair.
186. Mrs. Bumblebottom, a China Head with Spit-curls.

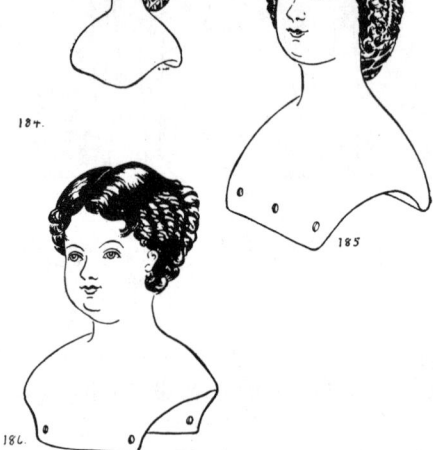

Juliette and Heather (184 and 185 respectively) are in the class with Lavinia. The doll snood is rare, and a long snood, such as Juliette wears, is still more rare. Heather also has a snood, just visible in the sketch. A band across the crown of the head terminates at either side with a rosette, from which hangs a feather. Both are china heads.

No. 186 is Mrs. Bumblebottom. Her claim to china-head distinction is the

Some Rare Old Dolls

187. Rosaline, a Parian Bisque circa 1880.
188. Eva, a China Head with Snood and Tassels.
189. Beth, a China Head with Rose and Medallion Decorations.
190. Princess, Parian Bisque with Snood on Crown.
191. Miss Verysmart, a Small China Head with the "Latest" Hairdo of 1868.
192. Front View of No. 181.

little spit-curl which branches out in a surprising manner at either side of the forehead.

Rosaline, contemplating the rose in her hair through a mirror (No. 187), is a Parian bisque circa 1880. She wears a molded blouse with a rosebud at center neckline. Ear-rings such as Rosaline boasts were most fashionable at this period, but few old dolls retain them. One can often find old jewelry, beads, etc., in antique shops which will answer the purpose. Another idea which has been utilized is the purchase of a necklace with pendants at the five-and-ten-cent store. The pendants are usually small enough to make ear-rings for dolls.

Eva and Beth (Nos. 188 and 189 respectively) are china-headed dolls of the pre-Civil War era. Dolls like these were later made in Parian bisque copied from the old china heads. It was easier to bring out detail in fine bisque than in china, but the fancy china heads are more rare.

Princess (No. 190) is a Parian bisque with white molded blouse and pink tie, circa 1860. There are many variations of this type, some with snood, some without, others with curls falling over the shoulder rather than the "waterfall," and still others with flowers or a wreath of flowers and leaves nearly encircling the crown.

No. 191, Miss Verysmart, has the "latest" in hairdos for 1868. She is a small china-headed doll, but her style is often seen in the twenty-or-more-inch size.

No. 192 is a back and front view of No. 181, a papiér mâché of distinction.

Nos. 193-198 are all Parian bisques with the exception of Elmira, No. 196, a rare china head of the eighteen fifties. Princess Junior, No. 194, with her graceful wreath of flowers and leaves, is an especially fine doll of about 1860. The others are later nineteenth century dolls. Nos. 193 and 195, Elsie and Ruth, respectively, have molded blouse and ear-rings. Grace, No. 197, is among the rarer of the Parian bisque dolls. Geneva, No. 198, is typical of the eighteen eighties.

No. 199, "Lady Hamilton," with the Gainsborough hat, is the only one of its kind the writer ever has seen. It is the same quality of Parian seen in the make-up of the finest Parian vases one finds in museums. In the shoulders there are the usual four holes with which the head is fastened to a cloth body.

No. 200 is an early rare papiér mâché belonging to Mrs. V. B. Dewitt of New Paltz, New York. Natural hair puffs have been added to either side of the head.

It is most difficult to find tiny china-headed dolls with fancy hair arrangement. No. 201, Carolina, is such a one.

No. 202 is a particularly fine quality of stone bisque from the Children's Museum, Jamaica Plain, Mass.

No. 203, a china with inset glass eyes, is highly prized by collectors, for this type is very rare. The doll belongs to Mrs. H. B. Plumb of North Hollywood. California.

No. 204 is a very fine old china "Jenny Lind." Most of this type are of coarse china with features not always attractive. This is the best of its kind.

Pansy (No. 205) illustrates the difference between the 1850 doll and the doll

193. Elsie, a Rare Parian Bisque with Molded Ruffled Blouse.
194. Princess Junior, a Rare Parian Bisque with Wreath of Flowers.
195. Ruth, a Parian Bisque with Molded Fancy Blouse.
196. Elmira, a Rare China Head with Snood.
197. Grace, One of the Rarer Parian Bisques with Molded Necklace and Braided Coiffure.
198. Geneva, a Typical Parian Bisque of the 1880's.

199. "Lady Hamilton," a Rare Parian with Gainsborough Hat. 200. Rare Papier-mache Belonging to Mrs. V. B. Dewitt of New Paltz, N. Y. 201. Carolina, a Small China Head with Fancy Hairdo. 202. Stone Bisque from The Children's Museum, Jamaica Plain, Mass. 203. Fine China with Inset Glass Eyes, Property of Mrs. H. B. Plumb, North Hollywood, California. 204. "Jenny Lind" of Fine China. 205. Pansy, a Parian Bisque of 1880.

206. Elizabeth, a Large Blond Bisque circa 1885.

Some Rare Old Dolls

151

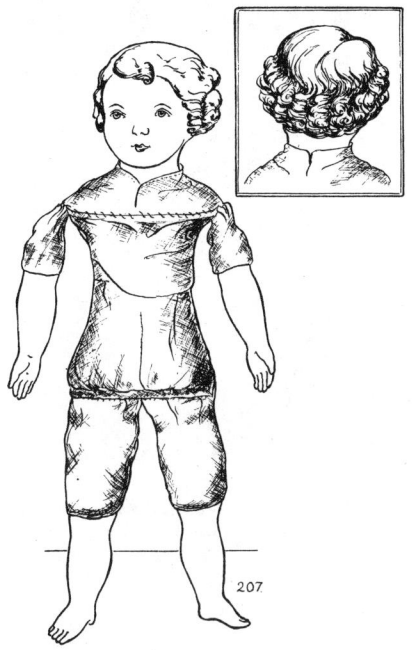

207. George, a Swivel-necked China Doll Sold During the Civil War.

208. Lady Belle, a Post Civil War Parian Bisque.

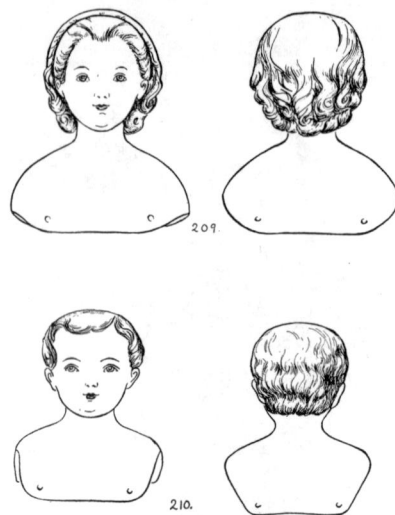

209. Alice, a Fine Quality Parian Bisque Doll. 210. James, a Companion Piece to Alice.

of 1880. The older one has longer shoulders and neck and more oval-shaped eyes.

Elizabeth (No. 206) is a large blond bisque (ca. 1885) with earrings. The original doll is exquisitely gowned in a blue velvet over-dress especially dyed to match the color of her eyes. The under blouse is of lace with a peplum, and the pink striped silk skirt gives evidence of past elegance.

George (No. 207, described in Chapter X) has a history that any doll might be proud of. Original baby clothes came with the doll, but they were taken off for the sketch in order to show the china legs.

Lady Belle (No. 208) is a post Civil War Parian bisque. The tiara, edged with a tiny gold band, is white glaze in front, black glaze at the rear. She is a well-proportioned twelve-inch blond, and came with original (although very much worn) basque dress.

Nos. 209 and 210 are a brother and sister combination, not easy to find in complementary sizes. Alice is a blond with a black back-comb. James wears a side-part. He also is blond, and both are the same quality Parian bisque with beautiful coloring.

No. 211 is an attractive music box doll owned by Mrs. Joseph Mallon of Philadelphia, Pa. The screw on the end of the stick fits into a groove inside the body, and by a flip of the hand, making the little fellow twirl, tinkling music is heard.

Jack is the young man (No. 212) who turns a neat sumersault over the back of the chair simply by pressing the lever at the right in the drawing. Doll and chair are of wood.

211. Music Box Doll Owned by Mrs. Joseph Mallon of Philadelphia, Pa.

212. Jack, a Trick Doll.

Chapter XIII

Reproduction Dolls

THE best reproduction dolls on the market at present, are those made by Mrs. Emma C. Clear of the Humpty Dumpty Doll Hospital, Redondo Beach, California. There are also cheap imitations which, unfortunately, have wrongly been credited to her. Recently the writer visited a dolls' hospital where some of the latter were on display. They had come indirectly to the owner of the shop, who jumped to the conclusion that they had been made at the famous Humpty Dumpty establishment. When informed that such was not the case,

213. "Jenny Lind," a Doll Reproduced by Mrs. Emma C. Clear of Redondo Beach, California.

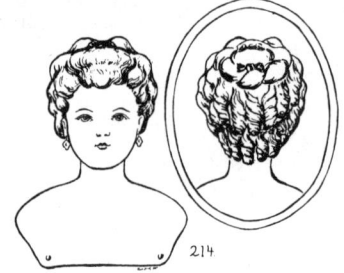

214. "Princess Mary Augusta," Reproduced by Mrs. Clear.

that the dolls she had could not compare in quality or workmanship with the fine imitations, the proprietor was surprised. "I thought," she said, "that no one but Mrs. Clear ever made reproductions!"

In buying collection dolls of this kind, it is well to look on the back of the shoulder of each doll. A reproduction by Mrs. Clear is plainly identified by the name printed on the back of the shoulder, as in Sketch No. 213—Jenny Lind—the first reproduction doll made at the Humpty Dumpty Doll Hospital.

No. 214 is "Princess Mary Augusta," No. 215, 19 inches tall; "Mona Lisa, Meisen Rose Lustre, Biedermeier Period, 1815-1840." This comes in two sizes, 18 inches and 27 inches; No. 216, "Augusta Victoria"; No. 217, "Little Kate Greenaway, Bonnet Doll, Parian," 13 inches; No. 218, "Claudia," 22 inches tall,

Some Fine Old Reproduction Dolls

Numbers 215 to 219 represent dolls reproduced by Mrs. Emma C. Clear. They are, upper left to lower right, "Mona Lisa," "Augusta Victoria," "Little Kate Greenaway," "Claudia," and "Parthenia." Mrs. Clear's dolls come in china, pink lustre, Parian bisque and blond bisque.

220. "Sir Galahad" 221. "Gibson Girl" 222. "Snooty" 223. "The Blue Scarf Doll"
224. "Barbary Coast Gent" 225. "Young Victoria" All Reproduced by Mrs. Clear.

exquisite blond bisque; No. 219, "Parthenia, Parian of exquisite texture, Grecian hairdo with three bands;" No. 220, "Dresden gentleman known as Sir Galahad, Parian of exquisite texture, 19-20 inches tall." This doll comes with a little pipe, mannish hands and boots; No. 221, "Gibson Girl, Parian, lustre flowers in hair. Corsage omitted on recent models." This doll is 18 inches tall. No. 222

226. "Elizabeth Parian" 227. "Dolly Madison" 228. "Spill Curls"; all reproduced by Mrs. Clear.

is "Snooty, the high born lady; Parian or Meisen Rose Lustre; pink or blue gold trimmed lustre bow on top of head;" No. 223, "The Blue Scarf Doll;" 17 inches tall; No. 224, "Barbary Coast Gent, made to order, size and material to match his little lady." The doll comes in three sizes, 12 to 19 inches, and in china Parian bisque, pink bisque or pink lustre. The old doll (late nineteenth century) from which this was copied did not have whiskers, goatee or "sideburns." A little pipe comes with the doll. No. 225 is described as "Young Victoria." It is 23 inches tall, "choice of china, pink lustre with black hair or Parian with blond hair." No. 226, "Elizabeth Parian," 22 inches tall, comes with painted or with oval glass eyes in the old style. Mrs. Clear has followed the lead of collectors in calling No. 227 "Dolly Madison." It is too bad that she did not have access to a similar doll (mentioned before) in the Smithsonian Institution, a doll which has almost the same hair arrangement, but has the longer neck and shoulders which usually denote the older china-headed doll.

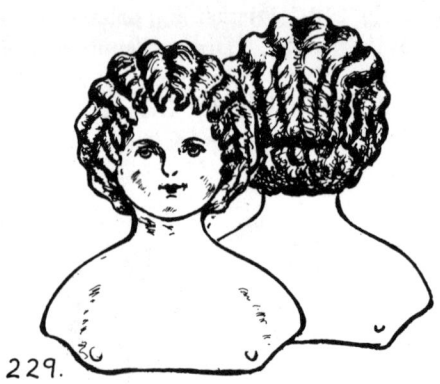

229. "Curly Top" reproduced by Mrs. Clear.

The latter really was made in Dolly Madison's time, the former in the 1880's. As Mrs. Clear explained, she uses the name the owner of the model gives the original doll. "They make convenient handles."

No. 228, "Spill Curls," 21 inches tall, comes in Parian bisque with gray hair or pink lustre with black hair.

"Curly Top," No. 229, also comes in china or Parian bisque.

Other dolls are Alice in Wonderland, Baby Stuart, Coronation Doll, Little Girl with Curl, Isabel, (Dresden with snood) The Grape Doll, Elsa and Toinette.

Reproductions are not the only dolls Mrs. Clear makes. There are some lovely portrait dolls sculptured by Martha Oathout Ayres, notably "George and Martha Washington," from the portrait by John Ward Dunsmore in the Metropolitan Museum, New York, N. Y.; "Danny," (Little Boy Blue) the artist's youngest son (hands and feet are modeled from life;) and the "American Madonna," portrait doll of a young mother.

At present, prices range from $12.50 for some of the smallest—12 or 14 inches—to $50 for the 24-inch handsome George and Martha Washington. Dolls with glass eyes are higher in cost than those with painted eyes, for antique eyes are scarce. For the ordinary factory-made modern glass eyes, the case is reversed. When visiting a doll factory, the writer was told that it cost less to have glass eyes inserted than to hire artists to paint the eyes.

Collectors who are visiting in California would find it worth while to make an appointment to see the Humpty Dumpty Doll Hospital and its miniature inhabitants, old dolls as well as new. Mrs. Clear says: "We usually have as many rare old dolls among our patients as you would find in a national doll show."

INDEX

Abigail, Mary 123
Adams, Abigail Smith 112
Adams, John 112, 117
Adams, John Quincy 116
Adams, Louisa Catherine 116, 117
Adams, Maude 110
"Aesthetics of Dress," The 142
A la Suisse 76
Alcott's "Little Women," Louisa M. 62
Alexis of Russia, Grand Duke 128
Alice 34, 36, 45, 104, 152
Alice in person 43
"Alice in Wonderland" 103, 104, 158
America 144
"American Costume," History of 47
"American Dolls in Uniform" 15
American madonna 158
American Red Cross 62
Ankle-length costumes 63
Anne 4
Antoinette, Marie 18, 98, 100, 101, 103, 106
Apron 62
Aprons 88, 89, 90
Arabesque patterns 57
Arabesques 51
Armature for small doll 15
"Art Journal", The 47, 142
Arthur, Julia 110
Arthur, President 129
Atrocia 26, 27
Atrocia becomes Cecelia 27
Atrocia, re-waxing 26, 27
Augusta, Princess Mary 154
Augusta Victoria 155

Autoperipatetikos Walking Doll, The Patent 110
Ayres, Martha Oathout 158
Babies' outfits 88
Back-comb 73, 74, 152
Ball dresses à tablier 56
Ball, General William H. 44
Ball, Private Robert Edward 45
Barbary Coast Gent 156, 157
Bareges, French 57
Basque 12, 63, 123
Basque outfits 40, 41, 42
Basque pattern 13
Basque, pointed postilion 65, 66
Basques 58, 63
Basquine 79
Bathing suits 61, 62
Bavolet 51
Beacon, Miss 145
Bean bag doll 2
Beatrice 96
Beecher, Henry Ward 83, 85
"Belle of the fifties," A 58
Bertha 50
Beth 147, 148
Betty, Miss 122
Biedermeier Period 154
Birch, Reginald 106
Blessington, Lady 48
Block printed face 4
Block printing 3
Blond bisque 150, 152
Bloomer balls 55
Bloomer costume 54, 55, 56, 76

Index

Bloomer, Mrs.	61
Bloomers	74
Blue Scarf Doll, The	156, 157
"Blue Boy," The	106
Bodice	53
Bodies	57
Body	62
Body making	37
Bombazine	41
Bonello, Pepito Costa Y.	106
Bonnet	7, 51, 58, 66
Bonnet doll	83, 154, 155
Bonnet pattern	9
Bonnet, poke	49
Bonnets	56, 57, 58, 63, 73
Bonnets, small	51
Bonnet, The evolution of the	50
"Boston Sunday Herald," The	68
Bouillonne	51
Bouillonnees	57, 77
Bouquets	57
Bowdoin College	124
Braids	63
Breton jacket	81
Brocade	57, 106
Bridal dress	58, 68, 69
Bridgewater, Miss	145
Bride and her outfit, A	70
Bride, White House	116
Bronzino's portrait painting	104
Brooke, Iris	47
Brown, Miss Margaret W.	109
Bruyere, Muriel Atkins	103, 104, 106
"Buds, Briars and Berries."	35
Bumblebottom, Mrs.	146
Brussels lace	50
Buchanan, James	124
Burke, Miss Fanny	114
Burnett, Frances Hodgson	106, 107
Buskin	144
Bustle	68
Bustles	63
Cabbage rose	74
Calcei	109, 141
Calico	73
Cambric	78
Camel's hair	86
Cameo broach	32
Campan's, Madame	115
Camp Fire Girls	3
Canagous	50
Cap	9
Cap pattern	9
Cape pattern	9
Capuchins	53
Cardinals	53
Carlotta, Construction of	21
Carlotta, Skirt pattern for	20
Carlotta, the clothespin lady	20
Carmago mantle	62
Carol, a china-headed doll	82, 83
Carolina	148, 150
Carroll, Lewis	103, 104
Carved doll, Parts of	16
Carving	17
Carving tools	16
Cashmere	79, 86
Casings	58
Catherine II of Russia	101
Cecelia, A dress for	28
Celicia	27, 145
Charles I	54

INDEX

Charles II	54
Charles-the-ninth cap	74
Chemise	79, 80, 81
Chemisete	51, 76
Children's Museum	148
Children's shoes	142
China doll with swivel neck	151
China, Emperor of	127
China head, brown-eyed with lower lashes	145
China heads, One of the rarest	146
China head with feather decorations	146
China head with hairdo of 1868	147, 148
China head with inset glass eyes	148, 150
China head with rose and medallion	147, 148
China head with snood	146
China head with snood and tassels	147, 148
China head with spit curls	146
Chine	57
Chinese	139
Chinese or pagoda sleeves	57
Chip bonnet	52
Christening poulaine	143, 144
Civil War	44, 59, 61, 62, 110, 113
Claudia	154, 155
Clay, Mrs.	58
Clear, Mrs. Emma C.	109, 154, 155, 156, 157, 158
Cleveland, Frances Folsom	130
Cleveland, Grover	130
Cloak	95
Clown	18
Cluny lace	78
Coiffure	58
Comedians	144
Constantinople	140
Coolidge, Grace Goodhue	136
Coral ornaments	50
Cording	73
Cornelia wrap	52
Coronation doll	158
Corsets	73
Costume Committee of the Smithsonian Institution	134, 135, 136
Courtesans	144
Covered wagon era	73
Crakowes	144
Crêpe lisse	86
Crinoline	50, 73
Crinoline hats	57
Curls	63, 73
Curly Top	158
Custis, Daniel Parke	111
Custis, Martha Dandridge	111
Dandridge, Betty Taylor Bliss	109, 122
Danny	158
Dante's time	96
Darling, Miss	82
Dauphin	106, 107
Decoration for boot or slipper	142
"De Deux Poupees"	82
"Delineator," The	1, 63, 79, 80, 81, 85, 140
Demi-evening toilette	68, 69
Demi-Polonaise	65, 66
Democratic Committee, New York State	138
Democratic National Committee	138
Derby, Mrs. Richard	133
Dewitt, Mrs. V. B.	148, 150
Dickie, a china-headed doll	83
Dinner toilette	60, 61
"Distinguished Women"	113
District of Columbia	114

Donelson	118
Donelson, Emily	117, 118
Dorothy, Carving of	17
Dorothy Dee, a French jointed doll	31
Dorothy, a wooden doll	16
Drawers	78, 80, 81
Dress improvers	63
Duchesse lace	119
Dugan, William	45
Dunsmore, John Ward	158
East Indian women	56
Ecru silk	51
Edith, a restored china-head	25
Edward VII, King	125
Egyptian	139
Eighteen century shoes	143
Eleanor of Toledo	101, 103
Elizabeth	150, 153
Elizabeth of Austria	96, 97
Elizabeth of England, Princess	130
Elizabeth Parian	157
Ellis, Mrs. Pearl Tyler	121
Elmira	148, 149
Elsa	158
Elsie	148, 149
Embroidered insertion	73
Embroidery for Mabel's petticoat	39
Empire period, First	47
Empress peplum	62
English costume	101, 102
English embroidery	74
English green	51
En soutane	61
Ermine	57
Etruscan	139
Eugenie, Empress	53, 58, 62, 101
Eva	147, 148
Evans, Mrs. Harry	118
Evening dress	53
"Evening Star," The	98
Evolution of the shoe	139, 141
"Exacto" blade	16
Executive Mansion	109, 111
Fall, Mrs. Sarah Polk	121, 122
Farmer satins	140
Fashionable colors	51
"Fashions for Early Summer" (1850)	56
"Fauntleroy," Little Lord	106, 107
Fawcett, Claire	16, 44, 46, 110
Ferrell, Mrs. Luta E.	85
Fichu	74
Fillmore, Abigail Powers	123
Fillmore, Millard	123
Findlay, Jane Irwin	119, 120
First Empire	142
Flat headgear	63
Flats	73
Flounce, Box pleated	86
Flounce, flower figured	123
Flounce, kilted	64
Flounces	52, 53, 57, 58
Flounces, Lace	56
Folsom, Frances	130
Foulard	62, 76
Francetta cloth	140
French bareges	57
Frans Hals	108
French costume	101, 102
French light silks	57
Frizzy bangs	68
Frock coat	50
French falls	144

French kid	140
Gabrielle	85
Gabrielle of Estrees	96, 97
Gainsborough	55, 106
Gainsborough hat	148, 150
Gaiter boots	73, 74
Gaiters	74
Galahad, Sir	156, 157
Gardiner, Julia	120
"Garden party Toilette"	68, 69
Garfield, Lucretia Rudolph	128
Garfield, President	128
Garibaldi blouse	70
Garrison, Mrs. William	133
Gates, Grandfather	138
Gauze	52
Geneva	148, 149
Genevieve, Collector's rag doll	10
Genevieve, Pattern for making	11
George	152
George, a modeled doll	20
George, Construction of	19
Geraldine	27, 29, 30
Geraldine, a jointed doll	29, 30
Geraldine in sixteen parts	30
Geraldine, Restringing	29, 30
German costume	101, 102
Gibson, Charles Dana	94
Gibson Girl	156, 157
Gigot sleeves	48
Gingham dress	53
"Girl Doll's Toilette"	80
Girl Scouts	3
Girl with curl	158
Glace silk	76
Goddard, Alice	34
Godey's "Lady's Book and Magazine"	47, 49, 77, 78
"Gone With The Wind"	103, 104
Goodwill Industries	47
Goodyear, Miss	145, 146
Gothic patterns	51
Gouverneur, Marie Hester Monroe	115, 116
Goya	106, 107
Grace	148, 149
Gracieuse	82
Granger, Mrs.	44
Grant	127
Grant, Julia Dent	127
Grant's Tomb	127
Grape doll, The	158
Greece	144
Greek women	56
Greenaway, Kate	71, 83
Greenaway, Little Kate	154, 155
Green, Mrs.	119
Guimpe	51
Guimpes	73
Guipure lace	57
Hair styles	111
Hale, Sarah Jane	113
Hamilton, Lady	148, 150
Hay, Mrs. George	115
Hayes, Colonel Webb.	128
Hayes, Lucy Ware Webb	127
Hayes, Rutherford	133
Half-bodies	73
Handkerchiefs, embroidered colored	49
Harding, Florence Kling	136
Harding, Warren G.	136
Harrison, Anna Symmes	120
Harrison, Benjamin	131

INDEX

Harrison, Caroline Scott 131
Harrison, William Henry 119, 131
"Harper's" 47, 51, 56, 59, 60, 77
Hats 57, 63
Haweis, Mrs. 142
Hayter, Sir George 73
Headgear 67
Heather 146
Heizer, Dorothy W. 96, 100, 101
Henrietta Anne of England 96, 99
Henrietta Maria of England 96, 99
Henry VII 139, 140, 141
Henry VIII 98, 139, 140, 141
Hermitage Association 118
Herrons 133
Hobble skirt 134, 136
"Home dress" 51
"Home Toilette" 59, 60
Higgin's ink 11, 37, 110
Honitan lace 50
Hoop, Decline of the 59
Hoop-skirt 58, 59, 105
Hoover, Herbert 137
Hoover, Lou Henry 137
Humpty Dumpty Doll Hospital 154, 158
Huntington, Daniel C. 128

Imitation Greek costume 142
India muslin 50
Infant doll dress 85
Infant's dress 85, 91
Isabel 158
Italian women 54

Jack 152, 153
Jacket 76, 83
Jackets, black lace 57

Jack's Fixit Shop 29
Jackson's administration, Andrew 117
Jackson, Andrew 118
Jackson, Sarah Yorke 118, 119
James 152
James, a china-headed doll 83, 84
James, Mrs. Julian 126
Japanese 139
Jean, before and after 23
Jefferson, Martha 109, 114
Jennie, an old papier mache doll 24
Jenny Lind 148, 150, 154
Jockey cap 50
Johnson, Andrew 126
Johnson, Eliza McCardle 126
Johnston, Harriet Lane 124, 125
Jordan, Nina R. 15
Josephine 52
Josephine mantle 52
Josephine of France, Empress 100, 101
Juliette 146
Jumeau 29, 31

Kean, Colonel Jefferson Randolph 113
Kestner Company 29
Knickerbockers 70, 78
Kangaroo shape 70

Lace 88
"Lady Doll's Toilette" 80
Lafayette, Madame de 115
Lane, Harriet 124
Lane, Miss 58, 125
Larkin, Mrs. Frances Hubbard 123
Lavelette, Mme. 104
Laver, James 47
Lavinia 146

INDEX

Lawrence 48, 108
League of Women Voters, The New York State 138
Le Brun, Madame 98
Leghorn hats 52
Leg-o'-mutton sleeve 68, 120
Library of Congress 73
Lincoln 110, 125
Lincoln, Mary Todd 110, 125, 126
Lincoln's aunt, Abraham 80
Lind, Jenny 110, 148, 150
Louis VII 106
Louis VIII 96, 99
London 55
Louise of Lorraine 96, 97
Louise of Prussia 100, 101
Lulu 65
Lynch, Anne Charlotte 52

Mabel 35, 36
Mabel (doll) 34
Mabel in person 43
MacDonald, Jeanette 68
Madame Royale 106, 107
Madison, Dolly 109, 110, 113, 114, 115, 130, 157
Madison, James 114
Madonna fichu 61
Mallon, Mrs. Joseph 152, 153
"Mamma in Miniature" 94
Manteau 51
Mantelets 51
Mantilla 52
Mantillas 53
Mantles 56, 57
Margaret of France 96, 97
Maria Theresa of Austria 96, 99

Marie de Rohan Montbason 96, 99
Maroon 51
Mary Ann 25, 26
Marie Therese Charlotte 106
Mary, Queen of Scotts 101, 102
McClellan, Miss. 59
McClellan's "History of American Costume," Elizabeth 47
McElroy, Mary Arthur 129
McKee, Mary Harrison 131, 132
McKinley, Ida Saxton 132
McKinley, President William 132
Meisen rose lustre 154
Mending Jean 23
Mending Jennie 24, 25
Mending Mary Ann 25, 26
Men's clothes 50, 96, 98
Merino 52, 59, 77
Merrifield, Mrs. 47, 54, 55
Mesopotamia 139
Metropolitan Museum of Art 101, 158
Mildred 45
Millais 106, 107
"Miscellany of Fashion" 140
Misses' costumes 73
Mitchell, Margaret 103, 104
Mitts, black silk 49
Moccasin 139
Mold, Making a 21, 22
Mona Lisa 154, 155
Monroe Elizabeth Kortright 115, 116
Monroe, James 115
Monticello 114
Montpelier 114
Moore, Miss Coleen 98
Morocco 140

Index

Mount Vernon 111
Morgan Memorial 47
Music box doll 152, 153
Muslin 52
Muslin body 77, 78

Nainsouk 76
Net 73
Night-dress 79, 80, 81
Nina 82
Norfolk jacket 70
Noyes collection 99
Noyes, Mrs. Frank B. 98
Nun's veiling 86, 88
O'Hara, Scarlett 103, 104
Opera polkas 57
Organdie 50
Osgood, Miss Susan 113
Overdress 63, 85, 86
Oxford College 131

Pagoda sleeves 51
Painting Jean 24
Panelled skirts 58
Panna Minutka 82
Pansy 150
Pantalettes 71, 72
Paper doll 66, 91, 92, 93
Paper dolls 68
Paper doll cut-outs 65
Paper doll cut-outs, Dresses for 67
Papier mache-headed dolls 145
Papier mache of distinction 148
Papier mache, rare 150
Parasols, small 51
Pardessus 51, 59, 61, 76, 77
Parian 147, 148, 154, 157, 158

Parian bisque of the 1880's 149, 150
Parian bisque of fine quality 152
Parian bisque, Post Civil War 150
Parian bisque with fancy blouse 149
Parian bisque with Gainsborough hat .. 150
Parian bisque with molded necklace 149
Parian bisque with ruffled blouse 149
Parian bisque with snood on crown 147, 148
Parian bisque with wreath 149
Parisian costume 78, 79
Parisian silks 57
Parting the hair 74
Passementerie 61
Patent Office 1
Pattern, Bonnet 8
Pattern, Cap 9
Pattern for Anne 4
Pattern for Genevieve 11
Pattern for Susie 6
Pattern for Tommy's costume 33
Patterns, Basque 13, 40, 42
Patterns for hood and cape 9
Patterns, Cape and hood 9
Patterns, Costume 4, 18, 33, 45
Patterns, Doll body 2, 4, 6, 11, 37, 45
Patterns, Dress 4, 8, 28, 40
Patterns for Robert Edward 45, 46
Patterns, Skirt 13, 20
Patterns, Underwear 38
Patterson, Martha Johnson 126
Patti, Adelina 110
Pelerine 76
Pelisse 59, 61, 77
Pendleton, Mrs. 58
Peplum 68
"Peterson's Magazine" 47, 62, 78, 79, 80

Petticoat embroidery	39
Petticoat era	49
Petticoats	58
PEO, Missouri Chapter	138
Pierce, Jane Appleton	124
Pigtails	73
Pike's Day School, Miss.	44
Pinkie	106
Pinkie, a bonnet doll	83, 84
Pique	77, 78
Plaid stockings	74
Plaits	64
Plumb, Mrs. H. B.	148, 150
Plush	37
Poinsett, Joel	122
Poke bonnet	68
"Polish braid"	50
Polish doll	82
Polka jacket	55
Polk, Sarah Childress	109, 121
Polk, James Knox	121
Polkas, opera	57
Polonaise costume, Misses'	85, 87
Pompadour sleeve	50
Pompadour style	51
Poplin	74
Parthenia	155, 157
Portland Magazine, The	49
Portrait dolls	158
Postilion	64
Post Civil War doll	148, 151
Postilion backs	58
Poulaines	142, 143
Pre Civil War	26, 148
Pre-Civil War doll	74
Pre-Civil War footwear	143
Price regulations	144
Princess	147, 148
Princess dress	38, 40, 41, 85
Princess dress pattern	40
Princess Junior	148, 149
Promenade costume	51, 60, 61
Promenade robe	59
Prunellas	140
Puffings	56
Pugh, Mrs.	58
Puritan, The	94, 110
Quaker	115
"Quarterly Review"	52
Quillings	57
Quilt	41
Randolph, Martha Jefferson	113, 114
Rag doll	1
Raphael Tuck and Sons Co.	68, 91, 92, 93
Rat-tailed shoes	143, 144
Rebecca, a china-headed doll	83, 84
Redingotes	50
Reed, Miss	59
Rehan, Ada	110
Reps	79
Restringing	29, 30
Revers	68
Reynolds	108
Ritchie, Anna Cora Mowatt	51
Romans	139
Rome	144
Robert Edward	45
Roosevelt, Anna Eleanor	137, 138
Roosevelt, Edith Carow	133
Roosevelt, Mrs. Franklin Delano	137
Roosevelt, Teddy	133

Rosaline	147, 148
Roselein	82
Roses en chine	58
Rosette	56, 75
Rostand's "Cyrano de Bergerac"	110
Rothschild, Master Anthony de	106
Rubber doll, A fine early hard	146
Rubens	54
Ruffled dresses	58
Russia leather	140, 141
Ruth, Baby	130
Ruth	148, 149
Sandal	139, 140, 141
Sanitary Fair	110
Satins	86
Scarf	52
Scott, Caroline	131
Scottish kilt	74
Scot towelling	21, 22, 24, 25
Serpent bracelet	50
Shawl	53, 58
Sea green	51
Sheridan, General	44
Shoe for Genevieve	13
Short hair	73
Sicilienne	63
Silks	57
Silly	18
Silly, Costume and pattern for	17, 18
Skirt adjustor	63
Skirt for Genevieve	13
Sleeves, leg of mutton	120
Sleeves to the elbow	73
Slippers	139, 141
Smithsonian Institution	99, 101, 109, 115, 134, 135, 137, 157
Snood	62, 146
Snooty	156, 157
Soccus	144
Sock	144
Soutache braid	86
Spartan patricians	144
Spill Curls	157, 158
Sports outfits	70
Spring pardessus	59
Stanford University	137
Stanton, Pauline	110
Stevens, Anne S.	49
Stocking doll	1, 2
Stone bisque	150
Stowe, Harriet Beecher	83
"Street Toilette"	68, 69
Stuart, Baby	158
Stuart, Mary	96, 97
Stuart, Princess Mary	106
Sunbonnets	73
Surah	88
Susie	6, 7
Susie, Bonnet and cap for	7, 8
Susie, Cape and hood pattern for	9
Susie, Pattern and dress for	7, 8
Susie's old dress	9
Su-su	17, 18
Symmes, Mrs. J. Cleves	118
Taft, Helen Herron	133, 134
Tassels	1
Taylor, Margaret Smith	122
Taylor, Zachary	122
Temperance journal	55
Tiara	58, 152
Tinkie	15
Thrift Shop	25, 47

INDEX

Throat band	59
Tight sleeves	68
Tight trousers	50
Timur the Lame	139
Todhunter School	137
Toinette	158
Tommy	32, 33
Tools for Re-stringing	30
Tragedians	144
Train	63, 70
Traphagen School of Design	101, 103
Trick doll	153
Truman, Mrs, Harry S.	138
"Transcript," The Boston	49
Trousers	83, 95
Trousseau costume	134
Tulle	57, 124
Tunic	74
Tunica	95
Tunica Talaris	95, 96
Turkish costume	55
Turkish woman	56
Turks	144
Twain, Mark	23
Tyler, John	120
Tyler, Julia Gardiner	120
Tyler, Letitia Christian	120
Tyler, Mrs. Robert	120
Udo	139, 140, 141
Undersleeves	74
Underwear patterns	38
Valenciennes lace	61
Van Buren, Major Abraham	119
Van Buren, Sarah Angelica	119
Van Dyck	54, 106
Vandyke-shaped neck	64
Velasquez	108
Venice	144
Verysmart, Miss	147, 148
Victoria	145
Victoria, Costume of	50
Victoria dolls	106
Victoria, Princess	71, 72
Victoria, Queen	50, 62, 145
Victoria's wedding gown, Queen	50
Victoria, Young	156, 157
Velveteens	86
Velvet poke	68
Velvets	86
Visiting dolls	82
Vogt, Miss Helen	98
Walking costume	51
Walking doll	110
Washington Button Shop	29
Washington, Colonel George	111
Washington, George and Martha	110, 158
Washington, Martha	104, 105, 111, 113
Waterfall hairdress	59
Watteau	105, 116
Waxing	26, 27
White kid	142
White satin boots	141
White House	110, 116, 119
White House hostesses	109
White House library	123
Wig making	5
Wilcox, Mrs. Mary R.	118
William II of Orange	106
Wilson, Edith Bolling Galt	134, 135
Wilson, Ellen Axon	134, 135
Wilson, girls, Margaret, Jessie, Eleanor	134

Wilson, Mrs. Woodrow	134
Winifred	14
Wooden clog poulaine	143
Wood for carving	16
Woolen dress goods	86
Worsted lace	57
Wreaths	56, 57